Getting to Know the Holy Spirit

A guide for new believers

Darren Edwards

Onwards and Upwards Publishers
Berkeley House
11 Nightingale Crescent
Leatherhead
Surrey
KT24 6PD
www.onwardsandupwards.org

Printed in the UK.

ISBN: 978-1-911086-12-3
Typeface: Sabon LT
Graphic design: LM Graphic Design

About the Author

Darren is an urban missionary and a church planter, based in Lincoln (UK), with the Elim Pentecostal Church. Living with his wife and two children, he lives a life of incarnational mission among unbelievers and new Christians. He is passionate about evangelism and discipleship  among unreached communities, and his church is affectionately known as Chav Church across the UK.

Darren's writing style is very easy to read for those that are new to faith. Although he did not complete mandatory schooling in the UK, he has achieved a B.A. Hons. Degree in Applied Theology with Regents Theological College.

Darren's background is one of crime and drugs, among other illegal activities from his youth, which drives his passion and mission to the outcasts — the lowest and least — in his community. His first book, Chav Christianity, has been discussed in many forums in the UK, and was written on the back of a dissertation about the class war's effect on the UK church.

Endorsements

Darren writes from his personal experience and his own study of the person and work of the Holy Spirit. He wouldn't expect you to agree with everything he says but this is a clear and plain Pentecostal guide for new believers. I'm proud to endorse this book.

R. T. Kendall

Darren has understood the secret of empowerment for all vision and ministry. As a pioneering church planter he has understood how important it is to lean heavily on the Holy Spirit. It is this empowerment that causes the weak to be strong and enables ordinary people to do extraordinary things. This book is highly practical and is particularly useful for people who are beginning their journey of faith.

Stuart Bell
Senior leader, Alive Church
Leader, Ground Level network.

In a day when there is a great need for an understanding of the person and power of the Holy Spirit, it is good to be able to recommend Darren's excellent book for new believers, 'Building a Relationship with the Holy Spirit'. I am convinced that all that read the truths contained in this book will be helped to grow and love life abundantly as described in John 10:10.

John Partington
National leader, Assemblies of God, Great Britain

Only someone as down-to-earth and honest as Darren Edwards could have written this book. His style is refreshingly honest – even sometimes to the point of making the reader stop to read again what he has just said – and that is exactly what I love about this book.

This is not a manual full of hypothetical theories, rather a record of the faltering success of a pilgrim travelling a radical road of exciting discovery with Jesus.

You may find this book challenging, particularly if you are like most of us, still carrying a touch of religion in our culture and approach to ministry, but be prepared to be challenged and rise above it! The dove is in the air and we are called to fly with him.

I commend both Darren and his book to you.

David Campbell
National Leadership Team, Elim Pentecostal Church

Dedication

I would like to dedicate this book to a great lady whom most people reading this book will not have heard of. I have no doubt that Dorothy Cave's name will be mentioned in heaven whenever my own ministry or life is talked about. Dot was part of my wife's home group for nearly three years before I committed to following Jesus, and she looked after my children in 'God Tots' at my home church.

Whilst regularly taking Dot to church, I was encouraged, challenged and believed in. Dot made me think that I could actually do anything, she taught me that grace goes beyond merely forgiving someone, and she taught me that no matter what is happening in life, there's always cause to smile.

I love Dot and I miss her. I'm sure that her name will be famous in heaven and that her days will be filled with joy and laughter.

God bless you, Dorothy!

Contents

Getting to Know the Holy Spirit

Introduction

Introduction

I'm a really keen evangelist, and I've spent a lot of time on the streets or working among people that don't know God. It's during these times that you soon start to realise how important it is to have a close relationship with the Spirit of God.

One day I was out collecting some furniture with my boss and church elder, Paul. I worked for a Christian furniture re-use charity. On this particular occasion we were out collecting furniture from a nice estate in our town.

As we entered the front garden of the client's home, I turned and said to Paul, "I think the person who lives here is a Buddhist."

Paul, almost jokingly, asked, "How do you know that?"

To which I replied, "I don't know."

I didn't want to say God told me and then be proved wrong, but when the lady opened her garage, she had a statue of Buddha on the floor in there. I asked if she was a Buddhist, and she confirmed it. When introduced to her husband, the Holy Spirit kept prompting me on how to best witness to these guys, and prompted me to ask a question that I could never have thought of myself. I'm pretty sure that Paul might have been a little impressed too. I think he hired me because I was evangelistic but had never really seen what I was doing until that point.

I asked the man, "Who decides whether you've been good or bad in life, and move up or down the ladder into your next life?"[1]

---

[1] Buddhists believe that when you die you come back as a different animal, or being, in your next life. Their end goal is to enter Nirvana – which is basically the end of existence, meaning that your life will finally end. If you are good in this life you will go up the ladder of beings towards Nirvana. If you are bad you will go down the ladder to become a worse sort of animal.

He could only answer, "There must be a judge."

To which I replied, "I know the judge; I could introduce you!"

Another time, whilst out with the van, my other colleagues and I went to deliver some furniture to a lady on a slightly rougher estate. As I walked into the property, the lady was quite abrupt and rude. Her face was pale and drained of colour, and she looked really angry. I didn't feel awfully gracious towards her. As she continued to be rude, I told the lads that I was going for a walk down the street to have a cigarette because she was "doing my head in". (I kept smoking after becoming a Christian, until I applied for Bible College.)

Whilst I was down the street having a cigarette, I felt the Holy Spirit tell me that I was supposed to be ministering to this woman, not having a cigarette; but I told him that I didn't like her. He told me to put my cigarette out and go and minister to her. I told him, "After my cigarette!"

He said again to go and speak to this lady, so I put my cigarette out and continued back to talk to her, but with a bad attitude. I turned into the worst evangelist and abruptly said to her, "I'm going to pray for you, is that okay?" To my surprise she said yes!

As I began to pray for her, the Spirit of God showed me a picture of abuse and so I prayed into that abuse and told her that God loves her. As I opened my eyes, she was crying and the colour had come back to her face. She was no longer angry and she showed me her arms that were bruised from abuse at home. Since this event, and one or two others like it, I have made it my mission never to say no to God again.

Both of these stories are from my early days as a Christian, before I went to Bible College; they could easily be the kind of stories that you could be telling people next week.

It was during my first year of Bible College that I started desiring to read more. One of the first books that I read was called 'Loving God Up Close: Rekindling Your Relationship with the Holy Spirit'[2], as I had a great desire to get closer to the God of heaven, who for the most part seems to be invisible. The Christian faith is based on a real relationship with a real God, but sometimes we struggle to connect

---

[2] Calvin Miller, *Rekindling,* ISBN: 0446530123.

with him in the way we would with our wife or sibling. My previous book, 'Chav Christianity'[3], was aimed at bringing the Christian faith to life in an easy-to-understand way. In my books I aim to explore faith through working-class eyes, and then share what I learn and experience with readers who may not be theologians and perhaps come from a non-Christian background. This may well be the first Christian book that you've read, but my hope is that you will understand it and put what you learn into practice.

This book is for you if you desire to build a relationship with God in a very real way. The Bible says that God is spirit, and so if we are going to meet with him regularly we must put effort into learning about God's spirit, otherwise called *the Holy Spirit*. Spiritual things can sometimes seem a little scary because we don't understand them, or because of the mystery. Even the most seasoned Christians can be afraid of spiritual experiences. However, in Luke 11 Jesus told his followers that God is better than any earthly father, and so if your earthly father won't hurt you by giving you a snake as a gift or stones when you ask for food, then your Heavenly Father will not desire to harm you either. Jesus said that God will give you whatever you ask for, assuming that as a Christian the first and most important thing that you might ask for is the Holy Spirit.[4]

I guess that a lot of people think of horror movies, or 'Most Haunted' and Derek Acorah, when they hear the words 'Holy Spirit', and so they tend to get a little scared. "What if I'm possessed and then he makes me do loads of crazy things?" The truth is that you are meant to represent God in everything that you do, and God doesn't want to come across as being crazy. In the same way that the writers of the Bible spoke specifically to their audiences (that's why we get confused over the meaning of some scriptures), God will want you to be culturally sane and relevant to your friends and neighbours. Remember, God only wants the best for you.

You may have also seen some stuff from the funky side of Charismania, and you wonder why people act a little weird in some Pentecostal or Charismatic churches. I've actually attended churches

---

[3] Darren Edwards, *Chav Christianity,* ISBN: 1910053945.
[4] Luke 11:13.

where people are so afraid of weird noises and so-called 'counterfeit expressions' of spirituality that they don't allow any of the expressions that we might associate with the Holy Spirit in their church. I always think to myself that these guys are so afraid of the counterfeit that they don't allow any space for God to move. It seems that in those cases the enemy – whether it's the devil or our human weakness – might have won the battle for freedom already. Let's not let the enemy win this battle in our lives!

So, as we go through this book, we will explore the Holy Spirit and who he is, as well as looking into why we need him and how we can get closer to him. My aim is that by the end of this book, you will be living life with the constant assurance that the Holy Spirit is both with you and in you, that you will know what it means to live a lifestyle of prayer and praise, and that you will be practising the same miracles and exploits that we read about in the Acts of the Apostles.

I pray right now that your faith will be brought to life and deepened, as we explore what life is like with the Spirit of God in our lives.

I

God's Spirit – Who He Is

One of the first things we need to learn if we are going to explore God is that some things are just a mystery. Everything that we know, every rule and guideline in the universe, was made by God. This means that he isn't subject to them. For example, God made time, which means that he isn't held captive by time. He can be at the beginning of time and at the end of time – at the same time! A little more simply put, if we built a program on a computer with certain rules and reactions, the computer will have to comply with all those rules, but we wouldn't. God made gravity but he doesn't have to comply with it; the Bible says that Jesus walked on water.[5] With this in mind, we can be thorough in our study and yet not fully understand or work God out.

If you think of God's Spirit like you would a ghost, then you're thinking of him through modern eyes. This way of thinking came out of the Persian Empire whilst the Jews were held in exile there. From what I understand about the beliefs of the people from the New Testament, Jews and other people groups of those times believed that angels and demons were in a constant battle to win God's favour. At the same time as hating humans for being God's chosen ones, they

---

[5] Matthew 14:22-23.

would try to do good things for men and women to win God's favour.[6] Most of our modern beliefs regarding ghosts and spiritual things would probably fall in line with what the writers of the Bible would have believed about angels and demons, but the Holy Spirit is someone else. He won't haunt a house, for example, and he won't possess a relic. He is actually God. If we can fully grasp what this means when reading about him, or building a relationship with him, then we can get lost in his mystery without being scared or worried.

This chapter will look through the Bible and other writings to find out more about who the Holy Spirit is and what he is all about. Let's start by looking at the *names* of the Spirit.

Holy Spirit

The Bible is made up of many different languages, most of which are now dead – that is, they are not used in the world today. They are kind of extinct! The main two languages that are used in the Bible are Hebrew and Hellenistic Greek, and the language of God's holy people was Hebrew. To get to grips with who the Holy Spirit is, we should probably look into the Hebrew meaning of the word 'holy' – *qadosh*. *Qadosh* means to be set apart for a purpose. In particular, it means to be set apart for God's purpose – used for no other purpose whatsoever. For example, if you used the sacred furnishings of the Temple for anything else but serving God, you would make them spiritually unclean. Therefore, the Spirit – and God, for that matter – are set apart for sacred purposes. The Spirit cannot come into contact with sin and he can't be used for personal gain. If you are filled with the Holy Spirit, then your life will most likely be fixed on serving God and him only.

If you're like me, then you will wake up thinking of God and how you will serve him; you may even wake up praising him because the sacred and sacramental things of the Temple were used primarily to give honour and *praise* to God.

When I first became a Christian, I promised God that I would serve him and be devoted to him no matter when he needed me. I gave him

---

[6] *Man and the demons,* http://www.sacred-texts.com/jud/jms/jms06.htm, accessed 4th March 2016.

permission to wake me in the night or call me out of work. I gave him all of myself and devoted my whole life to him. Soon afterwards I realised that God took my promise seriously, and I would often wake up in the middle of the night speaking in tongues or singing God's praises.

The other thing that I have noticed about my lifestyle and my desires is that I kind of hate sin. It repels me. When I first came into contact with God, I was really legalistic – this means that I would tackle people about their sin all the time and have a go at people about their behaviour. I dropped everything in my life that I thought was a sin, even setting my TV on fire at the bottom of my garden whilst my family were asleep. My wife came down in the morning and started screaming because she thought we had been burgled. I had to show her the melted TV to assure her that no-one had been in our home. I know – it seems a bit over the top. I didn't touch alcohol for nearly twelve months. I even stopped speeding!

However, holiness is not about keeping the law or setting TVs on fire. Holiness is a way of life that is God-honouring. Legalism divides but the Holy Spirit brings unity.

The Holy Spirit, then, is totally devoted to God and God only. If you are filled by his presence, you will also be separated from the world around to be devoted to serving God and his purposes.

Spirit of Jesus

It's important to know how the Spirit acts and what his personality is like, if we're going to build a solid relationship with him. For example, if we feel that the Spirit is asking us to tell a child that they are ugly, we might reconsider because we know that the Spirit is also known as the Spirit of Jesus. Jesus loves children, and telling them that they're ugly is a very bad way of showing love! With this in mind, I'd like to look at some of the other attributes of Jesus that might help us to know his Spirit more.

Jesus was *gentle* and yet he was *a warrior devoted to truth and justice*. The Holy Spirit will approach you like a dove and yet will cause a passion to arise in you for truth and justice.

Jesus was *gracious*. Just because something is true, it doesn't mean that it needs to be said. For example, if we look at how Jesus dealt with the woman caught in adultery, the truth was that she was guilty and that she should be stoned, according to the law of the Jews. Instead Jesus chose not to take offence at her sin, and he didn't follow through with what the law said he could have done. When I read this story I often feel as though the blokes that are standing there, with stones in their hands, are just bloodthirsty. They have no heart for justice, they just want to kill that woman. Jesus, though, wants her to be redeemed and restored, so although he recognises her sin, he doesn't condemn her for it but he encourages her to leave her life of captivity in sin behind. His heart is freedom![7] The Spirit is the same with us and through us. He wants us to be redeemed and restored, instead of condemned. When someone sins against us, they don't always want us to show them their sin. Sometimes they just want us to not take offence and to accept them back, thus restoring them into a right relationship.

To go through all of Jesus' attributes would be to write another book, but we'll cover many of them as we continue.

Spirit of God

God is known as the Father, and so in the same way that a child can learn his father's voice, we should be able to learn what the voice of the Holy Spirit sounds like.

In the Bible, Jesus said, "My sheep hear my voice." As any new mum knows, an unborn child can learn the sound of their parents' voices whilst they are still in the womb. It's the same with us and God. Although we can't see him, for the most part, we can still learn to hear his voice and differentiate between *his* voice and *other* voices that we might feel inside.

At our church we often practise listening to God's voice by sitting in a circle and relaying what we believe God might be saying to one another. We have one simple rule: that everything we say is positive. We tend to sit in a circle and then put our hands on someone, who will sit in the middle. We'll then say whatever we feel God might be saying. This could be dangerous in a group that is not managed well, because people often think that they have to trust everything they

---

[7] John 8:1-11.

hear. However, when we do it, we ask everyone who takes part to get up and tell the church what stuck out about what was said and how it relates to their life right there and then. The exercise isn't to prophesy; it's to give the person relaying God's message a clearer understanding of which voice is God's. After all, it is possible that we could relay our own thoughts or intuitions over a person's life, instead of God's message or voice.[8] The more times people relay the right message in our group, the more they learn to hear the voice of God, just as a baby would in the womb. Eventually, it is my experience that I can often pray prophetic prayers over twenty, thirty or a hundred people in one sitting, and get most of them right. Funnily enough, God's Spirit is also known as the *Spirit of Prophecy*.[9]

The Counsellor

Genesis 1 says that the Spirit of God was hovering over the waters of the Earth. The people of the Ancient Near East – where the Bible was written and took place – believed that there were many gods and that they would argue over the sea. This would create storms and innocent humans would be swept up in their fighting; some were killed or injured. I'm quite keen on science and for a long time I was really interested in evolution. Most scientists would say that at the beginning of time, as the earth was being formed, there would have been chaos. The seas would have been raging. This could be represented by the darkness that was over the deep. Genesis 1 offers the first glimpse of God's Spirit acting as a calming presence, hovering over the waters on the earth, like Jesus calming the sea in Mark 4.

Jesus told his followers that he was sending the Counsellor, otherwise known as the Holy Spirit, to help with life after salvation. I have found that life on our estate, and many other neighbourhoods, can often seem chaotic. However, just as Jesus stood up on a boat and calmed the storms of the sea, the Counsellor can often be the soothing balm that brings peace to the chaos in your life.

One of the first things that I did when I got to Bible College, in 2010, was to hang a picture of myself as a child and a picture of my

---

[8] Galatians 5:17.
[9] Revelation 19:10.

son next to each other at the side of my bed. For the three years following I would wake up and see my son, looking on him with love. I would also see myself as a young boy and feel the same sort of love and affection for myself. I had absolutely no idea at the time but later, when I left university and read a book called 'The Narcissistic Family'[10], I learnt that putting a picture of yourself as a child in a prominent place is a legitimate counselling technique. I became extremely emotional when it dawned on me that God's Spirit, the Counsellor, had caused me to do such a thing, to bring tried and proven counselling techniques into my life. It's true what they say: "All truth is God's truth!" God richly blesses his people with all sorts of doctors and psychologists, as well as his Holy Spirit.

Spirit of the Lord

When I think of the lordship of Jesus, I think of his authority. The word 'lord' means someone with authority, control, or power over others; a master, chief, or ruler. This is so exciting. Just imagine the impact if we could get to grip with what this means for our lives!

I spent a week in Kensington at a conference hosted by Reinhard Bonnke and a few other well-known evangelists in my third year of Bible College. One night, after one of the meetings, some friends and I were on our way back from doing some street evangelism, when we decided to stop at a Pizza Hut for some food. As we went to walk through the door, a member of staff stopped us and told us that they were closing. I asked if we could still have some pizza, but the staff member informed us that we were too late. It looked like there was no chance of getting into this place, and just as my friends began to walk on, I proclaimed, "But I come in the name of Jesus!" I only really said it for a reaction but this guy opened up the doors, sat us at a table and proceeded to give us his staff discount with free sides and drink. Amazed, and wondering if he was a Christian, I asked him about himself. It turned out that he was a Muslim and he was very keen to hear about Jesus. Now, if I can command the doors of Pizza Hut to open in the name of Jesus, then who knows what else we can do with the Spirit of Jesus living within us?

---

[10] S. Donaldson-Pressman & R.M. Pressman, ISBN: 0787908703.

One day I was sitting in our furniture charity van with my colleagues outside the house of a lady whom I suspected might need deliverance. Whilst I was waiting to go in, I felt the Spirit of the Lord within me saying, "The one who is in you is greater than the one who is in the world."[11] We prayed, and then walked into the woman's home speaking in tongues, at which point I greeted her with the gospel – telling her about Jesus, and the freedom that he offers – and told her to give her life to Jesus. We finished our work there and carried on praying for her after we left, to find that the next time we visited her she had started going to church with her parents.

The same Spirit that raised Jesus from the grave lives in you. He has authority over sickness, death, money, the weather and everything on this planet. So you have authority over sickness, death, money, the weather and everything on this planet! What are you going to do with it?

The Advocate

An advocate is someone who puts across another person's case, or someone who pleads in someone else's defence. The Bible speaks of the Holy Spirit making his plea to the Father on our behalf as through wordless groaning in Romans 8:26. In this way he is thought to pray for us, from within us; specifically, for the things that we need but might not be aware of. My wife has noticed me do this whilst I've been chilling with the kids. Some people get cold shivers and have even been known to gurn their teeth.

David Yonggi-Cho, a very well-known church leader in South Korea, explains this attribute of the Holy Spirit in a beautiful way. The Greek word used for the Spirit on this occasion is *Paraclete*, which can mean 'at one's side' or 'to call'. Cho explains that this word originated from court trials where a defendant was pressed so hard by the prosecutor that he didn't know how to plead for himself. The defendant might look around to find the familiar face of an influential friend. The defendant would walk through the crowd and stand next to his familiar friend who would then defend him and encourage him

---

[11] 1 John 4:4.

in order to win the case. This act of standing by him to prop him up and help him out was the work of the Paraclete.[12]

So the Advocate is your close friend and protector; he sticks up for you and helps to get your deepest needs and requests across to the Father.

Spirit of Truth

We are told to worship God "in Spirit and in truth"[13], and as I think about that, I start to wonder what it means to worship him with an honest and open heart. As I sit and ask the Holy Spirit what it means to be called the Spirit of Truth, I feel a sense of purity, like he is the Spirit of *pure intentions*. There is no malice or deceit in him, and he desires only the best for you. I often hear it said, "If God loves us then *why*?" But I believe that he is honest and does not have hidden motives when he says in the Bible that he loves us. Our understanding of love may be misguided, or our sense of justice and need to blame someone may be misguided, but the Spirit of Truth doesn't harbour any secret grudges or plans to harm you.

I've just been sitting with my son on the sofa, explaining why I put boundaries in his life. I told him that a shepherd often has to put a fence around his sheep, and that sometimes the sheep might wonder why they are trapped by that fence, but they never take into account that the fence also stops wolves from getting in. The Spirit of Truth doesn't hide secret intentions. He stays in the light; he *is* the light. There is nothing hidden in him or from him.

Spirit of Glory

I heard Kenneth Copeland speaking about the glory of God, and he described it as God's manifest presence. The apostle John claimed to have seen the glory of God in Jesus. As the Holy Spirit is actually the Spirit of Jesus, you can't get a much clearer view of the manifest glory of God than by experiencing what some might call

---

[12] D. Yonggi-Cho, *The Holy Spirit My Senior Partner: Understanding the Holy Spirit and his gifts,* (Lake Mary: Charisma House, 1989), 47.
[13] John 4:23.

God's *Shekinah* glory – this is, the restful dwelling of God's glory on earth.[14]

When I think of glory, I think of fireworks and an extravagant show of power and light. I can close my eyes and just imagine Jesus' face shining with a pure white light on the mountain top. I think of the emotional scene in the film 'Ben Hur' when the hero is being dragged across the desert and as he's about to collapse through lack of water, he sees a crowd gathered round a man. We never get to see the man's face but we know that it is Jesus. The centurion who is in charge of Ben Hur shouts and warns Jesus not to give the slaves a drink, but as the camera rests on his face, the centurion looks into the eyes of Jesus and all of his anger dissipates in a flood of glorious love!

Jesus is the Father's masterpiece, and so the Spirit of Glory must be his signature.

Spirit of Leadership

In Luke 4 the Spirit led Jesus into the desert to be tempted, but that's not where he stopped. The Spirit continues to lead *us*.[15] I know that in my own life the Holy Spirit leads almost all of the time in one way or another. It is because he hates sin that I hate sin. It is because of his love for the lost that I'm compelled to share the love of God with them. It is because of Christ's love for his bride that I have made the decision to never slag the Church off as long as I live. Deitrich Bonhoeffer claims that it is the Spirit that leads us to spend time with other Spirit-filled Christians. In fact, in his book 'Life Together'[16] he paints a picture of this being one of the first signs of salvation – the need to be around other Spirit-filled Christians. It is where we, like tools, are sharpened ready for work. The Bible says that Christians learning from each other is like iron sharpening iron, and so we should succumb to the Spirit's leadership if we are to be made fit for purpose.

---

[14] gotquestions.org, *What is the Shekinah glory?*,
http://www.gotquestions.org/shekinah-glory.html, accessed 8th December 2016.

[15] Romans 8:14.

[16] D. Bonhoeffer, *Life Together,* ISBN: 0060608528.

Spirit of Wisdom

After returning home on the day I committed my life to Jesus, I also got filled and baptised[17] in the Holy Spirit. I had done lots of research beforehand and I knew this was the only way to remain holy. When I got home, my first prayer was that the fire of God in me would never go out; my second prayer was that I would be wiser than Solomon. The Bible paints a picture that no man will ever be wiser than Solomon, but over the years I've found that relying on the Spirit of Wisdom when the right words and actions are needed can leave me in a good position to be seen as a rival for the wisest man in history. Those of you that know me will laugh because you know this is a joke, but my point is, "He that is in me is greater than he that is in the world."[18] I might not be the wisest man but I live a life in tandem with the Spirit of Wisdom, and he has no rivals!

Spirit of Judgement and Fire

Isaiah 4:4 says that God will cleanse the sins of his people with a Spirit of Judgement and a Spirit of Fire. When talking about Jesus, John the Baptist said that although he baptised people in water, Jesus would come and baptise people with the Holy Spirit and fire. He went on to explain that Jesus would judge the things that people had done during their life by taking them through what is commonly known as *the refiner's fire*.[19] The idea is that only your good works that are done to glorify God, not yourself or your own ambition, will survive the fire. These acts of goodness and kindness will be rewarded with treasure in heaven.[20] Everything else will be burnt up by the fire; the bad is like straw and the good is like gold.

The Spirit has the right to judge your intentions because he is so close to you, dwelling in you, and helping you to live a life that is glorifying to God.

Fire also speaks of passion. It wasn't long ago that I was speaking at a church in Worcester. I decided that I would be extra bold and

---

[17] See page 57 for more about being baptised in the Spirit.
[18] 1 John 4:4.
[19] Matthew 3:11-12; 1 Peter 1:7.
[20] Luke 12:32-34.

shout, "FIRE!" as I prayed over people, like I have seen on Christian television. My prayer before I went to preach that night was that God would do something amazing in my stupidity. After the service a man came up to me and told me that on this night he had responded to an altar call for the first time in thirty years. As I had shouted, "FIRE!" whilst praying for him, he had felt a hot oil run down his spine and his heart began to beat faster.

In our new church we have been trying to cultivate an organic spirituality. My aim is to simply preach the gospel, lead people to Jesus, pray for them to be baptised in the Spirit, and then live a life that is glorifying to God. I do this in the hope that I won't pass on any of the false religiosity that we may see in some areas of the church. Recently I spoke about the passion and fire of God, and asked if anyone would like to be filled with this fire. Several people were prayed for that night, and some of the things that happened in their lives included: (1) they began to read their bibles more and asked for us to start a Bible study group; (2) they became more passionate in their worship; and (3) they began to show gifts of the Spirit, like prophesying, tongues and a willingness to serve in church.[21]

My Pentecostal obsession of 'faith that works' draws me to the conclusion that this fire – the Spirit of Fire – gives us a passion for the things of God. It causes us to shout in worship, to speak wisdom and peace into our workplaces, and to move in supernatural ways among our family and friends. This same passion drives us to be better teachers, lawyers and doctors. I'm reminded again of King Solomon, who was given wisdom specifically to govern God's people. You might have a passion for administration that drives your company or church on to new horizons, and brings glory to God.

Spirit of Knowledge

Knowledge is different to wisdom in that knowledge relates to facts and stats that you may know, whereas wisdom relates to what we do with our knowledge. Wisdom is doing and knowledge is

---

[21] Often people look at tongues and the supernatural gifts of the Spirit, but don't pay enough attention to the gifts listed in Romans 12, of which serving is one.

knowing. The Spirit of Knowledge, then, has all the facts. He brings revelation into situations where there may be a lack of knowledge. It's important that we remember that he is God, he created the heavens and earth too. He knows what it means to have no beginning and no end. He is outside of time and space, and so he can be in three places at once. He is omnipresent – that is, there is no limit to his presence! He is omniscient – which means there is no limit to his knowledge! He has been in every environment and has been present during every struggle, which means that he knows how to handle every struggle and what to do in every situation. He is our ever-present comforter and counsellor. His presence is wonderful.

I have been around people that get worried at the thought of worshipping the Holy Spirit, but I truly believe that if you knew who he is, you would have no problems with bowing the knee to him. The Spirit is the weirdly physical yet spiritual embodiment of Christ and the Father on earth right now. As we begin to look further into his being and what he does in our lives, we'll hopefully be encouraged to find that he is our biggest fan, and that he's only too keen to share some of his passion, love and peace with us.

2

What the Bible Says

Our faith is often built on what we read in the Bible, and I get really excited when God speaks to me through it. This chapter will look at what scripture says about the Holy Spirit and the way that he acts, the way that he presents himself, and the ways that we interact with him. All this will be done with the aim of opening our eyes, and our lives, to new and exciting ways of interacting with God.

Over the past few weeks I've been seeing how God interacts with his children, specifically in our church in Lincoln, and I've become a little jealous. You see, during my walk as a Christian I've experienced God and his Spirit in so many different ways, and I love to know that he is near, but I get fired up and spurred on when the fireworks start flying. Just recently fireworks have been flying in our church – by which I mean we've seen God doing spectacular things such as healing and whole families or networks becoming Christians. But I've realised that I haven't had a vision, a dream or an amazing prophecy over my life for some time and I'm jealous for those things.

I want to look at how people who were filled with God's Spirit interacted with God. I want to see God face to face. I want to meet him in the flesh. I want to give Jesus a man-hug. I want to fly in the Spirit or transport from one place to another. I want to feel drunk with his presence and spend hours comatose whilst he works his way into the depths of my soul and heart. I want to be transported to heaven, to step through the cloud of light and to see his glory – his emerald throne, and lightning strikes, and the sheer power that would wreck me with awe. What's more, I want you to experience the sickening awesomeness of his presence and power with me. Oh boy, I'm ready for this chapter of my life – and of this book!

The Gospel of Luke

Luke is my favourite Gospel. I call it the Pentecostal Gospel because Luke seems to put every supernatural act down to the Holy Spirit. As you read through the Gospel you might notice a few things about the Holy Spirit's interaction with people.

Firstly, everyone who is filled with the Holy Spirit seems to be righteous; they keep the laws of God. We may be quick to analyse this information and to think that if only the righteous can experience a relationship with the Holy Spirit, then we are out of luck. However, we must remember that if we have put our faith in Jesus and have asked him to remove the burden of sin and shame, then we are counted amongst the righteous in God's eyes. You then, if you are a believer today, can also be filled with the Holy Spirit.

Secondly, every time that the Spirit is mentioned in Luke, there is some sort of action. The baby John the Baptist, still in the womb, jumps for joy at the sound of Mary's voice when he knows that the Saviour is near. Mary begins to worship with a song from the Old Testament, originally sung by a desperate woman whose son was going to serve the Lord. Simeon, an old man when Jesus was little, prophesies as he sees the Saviour of the world. Jesus himself is even sent out into the desert by the Holy Spirit.

I would love to go through every time that people experienced the Holy Spirit in Luke, but it would double the size of this book! So, for now I will just point out that when the Spirit is near, *things happen*. Sometimes they seem quite natural but a lot of the time those things are supernatural; either way, something always happens.

With this in mind, I feel a little grieved when some church leaders stand in front of the congregation and say that God is near when nothing of interest is happening. I feel that it often devalues the presence and power of God.

Skills and Abilities (Exodus 35:31)

There are times in your walk with the Holy Spirit when you will find that his presence causes you to do a particular job in a special way – maybe even a supernatural way. Take, for example, the musician in a church. For most of his time as a musician he plays well and the lyrics that he sings are quite uplifting or inspiring, but as the Spirit of God rests on him, one day he begins to play with a supernatural aura about him. One note can reverberate through your heart and one lyric can suddenly make you aware of God's supernatural presence. It is often the case in these times of praise that our mood goes from singing to worship; I've seen people healed and set free from emotional baggage without anyone even praying for them.

One such experience of my own was about two weeks into being a Christian, when I owned my own flooring business. I had taken on a job fitting some laminate flooring in someone's hallway, kitchen and living room. The hallway should have taken at most a day to finish, but God's presence was so thick around me at the time that I couldn't concentrate on work. I just wanted to sit in the middle of the room and worship him. I had to get my wife to come and help me by keeping me on track. It was whilst fitting a piece of wood under the stairs that I experienced God's Spirit giving me a supernatural skill. I had measured the piece of wood perfectly – or so I thought – to fit right under the bottom step of the stairs from behind. *But it didn't fit.* I felt like I heard a faint whisper telling me to trust God as I attempted to cut a new piece of wood to fit the gap. Instead of measuring, like I would do any other time, it felt as though God was quite literally guiding my hand as I cut the new wood with a jigsaw. To my amazement it didn't just fit, but it slotted in perfectly and the 'click system' held the wood together without any fuss. I knew right then that God had been with me in a supernatural way.

Sometimes things seem quite small or unimpressive, but if you can trust God to guide your hand in the small things, then he will teach you to trust him to guide your feet into the big things.

Courage (Judges 14:6)

One of the guys in our church recently shared a bit of the story of how he became a Christian and how life has changed for him. He told us all how for many years he had been afraid to leave his home and sometimes struggled even to walk to the shop alone. After meeting with God in our church, through the Holy Spirit's presence and power, he decided to commit to following Jesus and to ask him to be part of his life. This guy has gone from being afraid to leave his home, to now being able to walk into town and also into church by himself. He has gone from being afraid to walk round the corner to the shop, to being able to walk fifty minutes to church on a Sunday morning.

Courage isn't the absence of fear. Being courageous is doing what God wants of you in spite of your fear. In Gideon's story, Gideon wasn't just afraid of the enemy coming against him, he was afraid of his own inabilities. Yet God wanted to show his strength in Gideon's weakness, so he gave him supernatural courage by sending his Spirit upon him.[22]

You may be like our mate, who was living in fear of the people on the estate surrounding him, or it may be that you're scared of sharing your faith in the office, but when the Spirit of God descends upon you, there's a good chance that fear will be cornered and courage will take over.

Passion for God (1 Samuel 11:6)

When I think about being passionate about God, I think of Jeremiah 20:9:

> But if I say: "I will not mention his word or speak anymore in his name," his word is in my heart like a fire, a fire shut up in my bones. I am wearing of holding it in; indeed, I cannot.

An image of a burning house comes into my mind, and I can imagine a room with a fire inside, where the door is closed. I think it's called a flashback – when there is a fire in a room and it needs oxygen

---

[22] Judges 6:34.

to stay alive, so when you open the door the fire behind it explodes into the hallway. I can remember times when I've been in a church meeting or doing some street evangelism, and the Spirit of God has been tangible – like you can actually run your fingers through his tangible presence in the air. Suddenly I'll want to praise him or speak on his behalf, and it feels as though if I don't get this out of me, I'm going to explode. Opening my mouth seems to be like opening the door and I begin to shout. If I've got a microphone in my hand, you can almost guarantee there's a preach on its way. My heart begins to beat faster and harder. It feels like I can't get enough breath in, and I know – I just *know* – that if I don't roar, I might actually keel over and die. It's during these times that I often begin to praise and praise and praise some more! I was once told by a girl at Bible College that I was making her ears bleed, but I was sure that God would heal her anyway! I carried on!

When we pray for the Spirit of God to make us passionate, we often pray to be filled with the fire of God. I would pray for this every day, remembering all the time that it's passion for Jesus that I'm seeking, not passion for passion. I'm not interested in seeking goosebumps or jelly-legs, I'm seeking Jesus and him only.

Passion for the Lost and Hurting (Isaiah 61:1)

In the Gospel of Luke Jesus receives the Holy Spirit and then is guided into the desert, where he is tested with everything that we will ever be tested with: his identity is questioned; he is offered worldly affirmation (i.e. authority and splendour); and his faith is tested as the devil questions God's provision and calling. God's calling on Jesus' life is tested as the devil implies that Jesus will need food before he dies. However, Jesus knows that death isn't an option until he reaches the cross.

After this episode Jesus enters a synagogue, still full of the Holy Spirit, and quotes Isaiah 61:

> *The Spirit of the Lord is on me, because he has anointed me to proclaim good news to the poor. He has sent me to proclaim freedom for the prisoners, and recovery of sight*

*for the blind, to set the oppressed free, to proclaim the year
of the Lord's favour.*

My life, thoughts, actions and dreams were selfish until the day
that I was made complete with the Holy Spirit. It was at this point that
I was turned inside out and my whole life became about everyone
else. There's a great song, written by Hillsong, called 'Tear Down the
Walls'. Some of the lyrics are:

*This life is Yours and hope is rising
As Your glory floods our hearts
Let love tear down these walls
That all creation would
Come back to You
It's all for You*

*Your Name is glorious
Glorious
Your love is changing us
Calling us
To worship in spirit and in truth
As all creation returns to You*

*Oh for all the sons and daughters
Who are walking in the darkness
You are calling us to lead them back to You
We will see Your spirit rising
As the lost come out of hiding
Every heart will see this hope we have in You*

There have been times, as the Holy Spirit begins to manifest, that
I've found myself with tears in my eyes beating on the walls of the
church, praying that God would remove the stone blockage between
us and the world that is in pain around us. Others show their passion
through remaining faithful to God during really tough times. For
example, Mother Teresa spent a long time living and working in a
leper colony, serving the poor and needy.

Physical Yet Spiritual Presence (Matthew 3:16)

As I was going through my bible looking for scriptures where it mentions the Holy Spirit interacting with people, I came across Matthew 3:16. I was intrigued because it seems that several people saw the Spirit descend on Jesus like a dove. Matthew goes on to say that the Spirit *alighted* on him – the Greek here means to come and enter him, in the present tense. In other words, the Spirit *stayed with him*. This is almost the same as in Acts 2, where Luke tells his readers that tongues of fire came to rest on the disciples' heads. So, what looked like a physical dove[23] came down from heaven.

Reading this scripture reminded me of a time when a friend, Sam, and I were shopping in Morrisons. Sam had been meditating on Acts 2 and was talking to God, asking him why we don't see tongues of fire in church. He was clearly feeling as though he wanted more. Sam wanted to see fireworks in his walk, too. Then, out of the blue, a little boy in a pram turned to his mum in hysterics. Laughing, he proclaimed, "Look, Mummy, those men have fire on their heads!" Maybe, just maybe, the Spirit of Jesus is more physical than we give him credit for. If only we could see the things of the Spirit more clearly.

You can pray for this: "God, let me see you as you work and hear you loudly when you speak!"

He Directs Us (Matthew 4:1)

Throughout the New Testament we read of times when God's Spirit has guided people; even stopping the apostle Paul from going to some places. But although he is known for guiding people, Christians often put too much emphasis on waiting for God's 'yes'. When I read the Bible, I see lots of stories of God sending people to places, but I don't see any examples of people waiting for God's direction. Christians tend to act as if waiting for direction is wise, when God has already given them direction through the Bible. "Be holy."[24]

---

[23] It's worth noting that the Spirit may not have *looked* like a dove, but may have been *acting* like a dove. He could have looked like a physical human or a shadow.

[24] Hebrews 12:14.

"Influence others."[25] "Preach the gospel."[26] With this in mind, it is less about waiting for God's direction and more about doing what he says.

However, there are times when the Spirit of Jesus meets with you in a special way and he quite literally tells you to go to a certain place, maybe to speak to a particular person.

We've been known to go 'treasure hunting'. This is when you spend some time in prayer asking God's Spirit to give you directions to people that you can witness to (i.e. asking God for the treasure). As God gives you information – like names, places and what people are wearing – you write them down. Say, for example, that two people in the room feel God is saying the name 'Ethel' and that she is wearing a black coat and has a cast on her arm. You would put that information as a priority on everyone's notes. Then you head into town to try to find your treasure – a lady wearing a black coat, near McDonalds, with a cast on her arm – and when you find her, you introduce yourself as looking for a lady of her description named Ethel. At which point, if her name is Ethel, you show her your notes and begin to speak into her life because she is now open to the gospel. This is an extremely effective way of sharing your faith through the prophetic. Maybe next time you're feeling a little bored, or looking for ideas to share your faith, you might ask the Spirit of Jesus to guide you towards your very own Ethel.

He Speaks Through Us (Matthew 10:20)

If you've been a part of any Pentecostal church in the past, you will be used to someone standing up and speaking out a word of prophecy. In an ideal world it would always be the case that the Holy Spirit has spurred that person to speak on his behalf. However, you should always check that what is being said falls in line with God's character.

In recent times some of the people in our church have told me that when they first came to church, they felt as though I was answering every question that they had about God without them asking. For some, this is what convinced them that God was real and that he was

[25] Matthew 28:19.
[26] Mark 16:15.

active in our meetings. They were converted to following Jesus by the prophetic uttering of the Holy Spirit as I spoke, even if I knew nothing about it.

This kind of prophetic preaching isn't a new thing either. Whilst I was doing a work placement during my third year of Bible College, a man from my home church sent me a typed copy of his journey to Christ. He was well into his seventies, maybe even his eighties. He said that the first time he went to a church, when he was very young, he visited a Pentecostal church. He claims that it felt as though he was the only person in the room and that the preacher was speaking directly at him. The speaker seemed to have read him like an open book.

We should be more confident in our calling and in the anointing that God has placed upon us. I've never felt as confident as I do now that when I talk, I am truly speaking on behalf of God, and people will just become convinced of God when I do.

You May Speak in Tongues (Acts 2:4)

As you read the book of Acts, you may notice that the majority of times that it mentions followers of Jesus being baptised in the Spirit, it is followed by them speaking in tongues. If you've ever wondered what tongues are, it gives one example in Acts 2. There it says that Jesus' disciples spoke in foreign languages that other people could understand, even if the disciples themselves couldn't. Tongues are also widely known as the language of the angels, or 'the heavenly language', as found in 1 Corinthians 13.

If you're anything like me, you might feel a little self-conscious about speaking in tongues if you haven't done so before, but let me encourage you that when you do you will feel absolutely brilliant. The Bible says that speaking in tongues edifies us. This means that it confirms to us that we are Christians filled with the Spirit of God. If you're feeling a little shy but know that God may have given you this gift from heaven, best would be to find somewhere that you can put your favourite worship songs on really loud, and worship until all you have left is what sounds like a foreign language. Then speak it out. You may speak it softly or you might want to shout it. Be passionate with it and then practise it whenever the Spirit leads you to.

There are other gifts of the Spirit that I'll mention later in this book.

You May Feel or Look Drunk (Acts 2:15)

Another thing that was mentioned in Acts 2 is the fact that the disciples looked drunk. Some people even laughed at them for being drunk. The apostle Paul instructs the churches in the New Testament to not get drunk on wine but instead to get drunk on the Holy Spirit. That wasn't Paul eluding to a bunch of monks that were brewing vodka, but the feeling of drunkenness when the Holy Spirit is manifesting in your presence. I can almost imagine the disciples of Jesus stumbling around or lying on the floor giggling, as the Holy Spirit replaced their grief and fear with perfect love.

There are some things that happen in Christian circles that might look a little similar to that day in Acts 2. One of our guys at church recently began to experience the Holy Spirit for the first time. He claimed that his legs went like jelly and he had to sit down for a while. If you looked at him, you'd think he had drunk a bottle of whiskey halfway through the church meeting. I've seen people having to be carried away from the pulpit because they can't stay on their feet, and I've also seen the equivalent of people not being able to handle their drink as they roll around on the floor and make some silly noises.

You May Be Supernaturally Transported (Acts 8:39)

I love to have a bit of a laugh, especially with the lads, and we often go to Bradford for a huge men's conference in November. I think one of the funniest moments we've had together was a few years back, when I went to Life Church with five or six mates. Let me paint a picture for you, just in case you've never been there. The church sits near the top of a really steep hill, at the bottom of which is a retail park with a McDonalds on it. There's also a great little Indian next to the retail park, that I'm not sure all of the men know about. So, during our lunch break at the men's conference, everyone runs down the hill to descend on McDonalds, and if you're a blokey bloke like me, you'll munch a little extra just because the wife isn't there to stop you. This particular time I was with some slightly competitive friends and I had decided to get an extra double cheese burger. You know how sluggish you feel after you've eaten a bit too much; as I walked out of Maccy D's, I lifted my head to see the huge hill to climb, and it hit me – I had to climb back up that with a full stomach. Remembering the story of Philip the Evangelist,[27] I thought, "I'm an evangelist. Maybe I can be transported in the Spirit!" Closing my eyes intently, I prayed a fervent prayer that I would not have to do that hill climb and, as I opened my eyes, I was absolutely amazed to see that... I hadn't moved an inch! I tried a couple more times but the lads just laughed at my constipated look and we had to walk it anyway.

However, there is a man by the name of Brother Yun who tells amazing stories of being transported in the Spirit and of being set free from jail in modern China.[28] His story is gripping and inspiring. I really do believe that the Bible offers just a small glimpse of what can be done when the Spirit is moving. Maybe we should expect more and doubt less.

You Will Raise People from the Dead (Acts 9:40)

For all the fun and joking as a Christian, we can often forget just how powerful God is. I've made it my mission to remind Christians that God is massive. Nothing is impossible for him. Before I came to Lincoln I joked with friends saying that we were going to start the zombie apocalypse by raising people from the dead – like we see in so many other countries. A guy in our church recently asked how he would know he was filled with God's power. Jokingly I told him that we'd know if he was filled by the amazing, supernatural, powerful Holy Spirit if he started raising people from the dead in the morgues, and that no other sign or wonder would do – all in jest, obviously. It sounds ridiculous to some people that we actually believe this could happen, but we hear of people in Africa being raised from the dead all the time, and in the Bible it says that when Jesus died and the Holy Spirit broke free, hundreds of people came back from the dead.[29] Nobody prayed

---

[27] Acts 8:4-12.

[28] Brother Yun & P. Hattaway, *The Heavenly Man: The remarkable true story of Chinese Christian Brother Yun,* (Oxford: Monarch Books, 2002), 38-39.

[29] Matthew 23:52-53.

for them. Just the sheer unlimited power of God's Spirit rose people from the dead that were anywhere near the blast radius. Oh boy! I want that unlimited power to grace my life! I want to create a culture of belief in our nation that says, "Anything is possible!"

We joked when people asked how our church would be funded, by telling them that we'd sell the crutches and wheelchairs that people left after they'd been healed. *Lord, bring them in! We want to see amazing things in our life! We're bored of listening to other people's stories!*

You Will Be Led to Meetings (Acts 9:11-19)

I love the story of Paul's conversion, and I really love the part where Ananias is led to meet Paul in the house of Judas.[30] It reminds me of a story I've heard of Brother Yun who, after receiving salvation from God, begged him for a bible for months and managed to memorise loads of it really quickly once he received it. He was so desperate for God and keen to serve him that one night God gave him a vision of people that were fasting and praying for God to send the young man to their village to preach the gospel. The Holy Spirit actually showed Brother Yun a young man in a vision and told him his name. He then showed him villages that he needed to visit in order to preach the gospel. The next day he went and recited the Gospel of Matthew to the people of the village and about forty people gave their lives to Christ.[31]

I've also heard a story of someone shouting, "Jesus loves you!" through a letterbox after being prompted by God over a few days. He then found out that the person living inside the house had been about to hang themselves because they felt lonely. That person went to church and committed to follow Jesus, and eventually fell in love with him, all because that person had called through a letterbox.

If we commit to being obedient to God, he will give us opportunities to do amazing things and make history.

---

[30] Acts 9:10-17.
[31] Yun & Hatherway, *The Heavenly Man*, 35-40.

Holy Laughter (Acts 13:52)

I was always a little sceptical of the notion of 'holy laughter' – until one night before I came to Lincoln. A friend and I were staying in a hotel, and as we were going to sleep, it felt as though there was a 'bad feeling' in the room. I don't know how to describe the feeling, other than to say that it felt a bit awkward, maybe a little anxious in there, and maybe scary too. I had felt this feeling once before and I was pretty sure that it was something demonic in the atmosphere. You hear stories all the time about what goes on in hotels and so it wouldn't surprise me if there *was* something demonic. I asked my friend how he was feeling and to my surprise he felt the same. So we decided to pray about it and ask God's Spirit to fill the room that we were in and to give us peace. After all, we had a long day ahead in the morning.

As we began to pray together, I closed my eyes and saw a vision of a room filled with thick darkness and, as we prayed, a light came in from one side of the room and pushed the darkness out. When this happened, the feeling of dread seemed to dissipate and the room was filled with what I can only describe as *Holy Spirit joy*. We both burst out laughing at the same time, and my friend even started speaking in tongues. Needless to say it took a little while to get to sleep, but this time it was because we were both so excited about the Spirit's presence, and we were overawed by this awesome sense of fun, joy, and laughter.

You Will Ooze the Spirit (Acts 19:12)

I've been so intrigued by what the Holy Spirit does that I've come to the conclusion that he's unfathomable. In this particular verse in the Bible, the disciples of Jesus seem to ooze a powerful aura of healing, so much so that as their shadow passes over people, healings begin to take place. The things that the disciples touch seem to have a healing power in them. As I've meditated on this amazing occasion, I can't help thinking that we as disciples of Jesus are not powerful and our clothes certainly have no power in them. Surely this power that seemed to go beyond their touch can only be that of the Holy Spirit!

I was in Tewkesbury helping to minister at a small church for a few months whilst I was at Bible College, and during one of our healing services some amazing things began to happen. One man even emailed me a month or so later claiming that he had been healed from cancer. That was quite exciting, but what grabbed my attention more than anything else was what a seemingly well-rounded lady said about the Holy Spirit after one service. In an email sent to me a few days after the meeting, she said that it felt as though the Spirit of joy and of peace was flowing from our church building, like a river that was flooding the streets.

When I talk about the baptism in the Spirit at our church, I often liken our lives to a sponge and the Holy Spirit to water. The meaning of the word 'baptism' is to be saturated; as our sponge is saturated in the Holy Spirit, God guides us with his hand and spills his Spirit over everyone and everything that we come into contact with.

If you've been reading the Bible verses that I've mentioned in this chapter, you might notice that I've put my own slant on them; I've paraphrased each one in order to try to make sense of it a little more. You will also notice that I've related them to personal stories from my own life and ministry. This is because it's important to see that the Holy Spirit's interaction with us didn't stop two thousand years ago, and God isn't limited to what the Bible says about him. People don't only get healed in Israel, and they're not only raised from the grave in Jerusalem. God inhabits the whole earth and will continue to move wherever his praises are heard.

3

Interacting with Him

Although God's actions and interactions with us are not limited to what we read in the Bible, his justice, morals and personality will never change from what we see in the scriptures. This means that God will always be good; he will never be bad or wicked. His heart will always be for saving life and so he'll never instruct you to take a life. He will always be the bringer of peace and joy, so he's not going to suddenly start tormenting you.

With all of this in mind, this next chapter will look at the experiences of people outside of the Bible to widen our scope of experience and interaction with God's Spirit. Some of the things in this chapter may be seen as controversial, and others might seem totally unbelievable, but the aim here is to expand our faith. That said, it is important to test the motive behind the actions of people around you,[32] and keep in mind that there is a very real enemy who desires to dampen your faith with counterfeit actions. My personal view is that I'm happy to attribute most things to the Holy Spirit, on the condition that whatever is happening doesn't take the focus away from God and the gospel if it is being preached. So, if someone is shouting and screaming whilst the general atmosphere is one of peace or the speaker has begun to speak, I would be inclined to remember that the

---

[32] 1 John 4:1.

Holy Spirit brings order to chaos. We can be secure in the knowledge that the Holy Spirit will not lead us to do anything that is unscriptural.

This said, it's time to delve into the past and present, to broaden our relationship with the Spirit of Jesus.

The Blazing Church – Francis of Assisi

In his book 'Streams of Living Water', Richard Foster writes about Francis of Assisi:

> *Because of the striking power in the Spirit that surrounded all that Francis did and said, perhaps one story will suffice...*[33]

Foster goes on to tell the story of a meeting between St Francis and St Clare, a colleague from the order of St Francis. The story starts with these two followers of Jesus eating a meal in really humble circumstances – like poor people – at which point they begin to talk about God in a special way. I imagine them to be praising God. The story goes on and it is mentioned that the two become "rapt in God". I can only imagine that they became quite excited, yet peaceful; consumed by the Spirit's presence. Then, all of a sudden, the people in the village at the bottom of the hill from where they were staying saw the church that the saints were meeting in, and all the forest surrounding them, on fire. The villagers were so horrified that they rushed up the hill with the aim of putting out the fire, but when they arrived they found that neither the church nor the forest were on fire at all. Foster remarks:

> *The fire they had seen was not a material fire, but a spiritual fire. The blaze they saw was 'to symbolize the fire of divine love which was burning in the souls' of these simple servants of Christ.*[34]

Imagine that – being in a room that was so filled with God's Spirit that people outside actually thought that your building was on fire.

---

[33] R. Foster, *Streams of Living Water: Essential practices from the six great traditions of Christian faith*, (New York: Harper Collins Publishers, 1998), 100-101, ISBN: 0060628227.
[34] ibid.

The closest I think I've ever come to that sort of feeling is once when I was fasting and praying, when a friend came into the chapel where I was chilling with God and remarked at how they could feel the thick presence of God as they walked through the door. To be honest, I'm a little jealous of Francis of Assisi and his friends – and maybe you should be too. Whilst being aware that we are creatures of habit, let me just encourage you to get into the habit of seeking God's presence with praise on your lips, and love or grace in your heart. There's nothing more exhilarating than getting wrapped up in praising the God that created you and upholds you.

Carpet Time – Toronto Blessing

In 1994 the world saw a new era emerge with the start of a certain church in Toronto, Canada. Thousands would flock to this church with a desire to receive a blessing from the Holy Spirit, and as they did so, followers of the movement began to witness the phenomenon of a manifestation nicknamed 'carpet time'.[35] As people were prayed for at the front of the church, during a period commonly known as 'ministry time', they would often fall over under the power of the Holy Spirit. At the time of the movement's conception this confused onlookers because they struggled to find anywhere that this was mentioned in the Bible. Over time, however, some of the biggest critics of the Toronto Blessing have resigned to the understanding that over time lives have been changed and people have become more holy – a sure sign of the Spirit's presence. Writer of the critical book 'Holy Laughter and the Toronto Blessing', James Beverley, recently said:

> *Whatever the weaknesses are, they are more than compensated for by the thousands and thousands of*

---

[35] J. A. Beverley, *Holy Laughter and the Toronto Blessing: An investigative report,* (Grand Rapids: Zondervan, 1995), 16; L. Dueck, Christianity Today, 'Enduring Revival', ISBN: 0310204976, http://www.christianitytoday.com/ct/2014/march-web-only/enduring-revival.html, accessed 20th September 2014.

> *people having had tremendous encounters with God,*
> *receiving inner healings, and being renewed.*[36]

Needless to say if many people have experienced this blessing and have come out of it with a renewed sense of holiness and inner healing, then there is a good chance this is of God. To explain this act of falling over under the power of the Spirit in our church, I draw attention to Acts 2, where people thought that the disciples of Jesus were drunk when filled with the Holy Spirit. I ask the question, "What happens when you're drunk, and what must it look like to be drunk for these onlookers to draw that conclusion?" My answer would be that if you go into town on a Friday night, you'll find people stumbling around, falling over, and generally looking a little worse for wear. They might slur their words and they might even act a little foolishly. I certainly wouldn't be surprised to find people lying on the floor asleep. Furthermore, I draw attention to the fact that often people need what I would call 'spiritual heart surgery'; God needs to put people under 'spiritual anaesthetic' in order to carry out his work in renewing our minds and lives.

An American Enters the Dome on the Rock – Todd White

In terms of Holy Spirit stories, this one is particularly good because you don't have to take my word for it. You can actually buy a DVD and watch this story play out for yourself. In recent times a film producer called Darren Wilson has embarked on a mission to film the Holy Spirit at work; on this particular occasion he managed to catch an amazing story on film.[37]

If you know anything about Middle Eastern politics and religion, you'll be aware that it is hard to get into the Dome on the Rock, in Jerusalem, if you are not a Muslim. It's nearly *impossible* to get into the ancient building if you are a Western infidel. In his film, Darren Wilson introduces a wild evangelist by the name of Todd White, who

---

[36] L. Dueck, Christianity Today, *Enduring Revival*, http://www.christianitytoday.com/ct/2014/march-web-only/enduring-revival.html, accessed 20th September 2014.

[37] You can watch the story on the documentary 'Father of Lights'. Reading it is one thing, but seeing it is another.

takes it upon himself to show the power of the Holy Spirit by trying to get into the Dome on the Rock, where the Holy of Holies is said to be. His aim is to worship God and invite the Holy Spirit's presence into the place that he once called home.

Todd enters Jerusalem with the aim of just praying for people as he walks through the streets. On his travels he tends to see many people healed and he is really prophetic in his style of evangelism. One of the first guys that he meets in the city is a large man wearing a yellow T-shirt. Todd prays for this man, who is miraculously healed, and then goes on his way. As he carries on witnessing, making his way through Jerusalem, many people are touched by the power of God.

Eventually Todd finds a Christian man who invites him home to pray for his father-in-law. After praying for this guy's dad, Darren asks the question, "How can I get into the Dome on the Rock?" to which the man explains that it's impossible, but that he might know a friend that can help. He leads Darren and Todd through Jerusalem to meet his friend, who may well be the only person in Jerusalem that can get an American into the highly religious centre for Muslims. The camera angle as they approach this guy's friend is brilliant. As Darren films from behind their new friend, leading Todd down the street, there seems to be utter amazement ahead of the camera as from in front of Todd White emerges... the man wearing a yellow T-shirt! Soon everyone is hugging and high-fiving!

(As I watched the video, my chest started hurting as my heart began to race the fastest I'd ever felt it. I was absolutely amazed at how awesome God is.)

As this guy has been healed earlier, he's really open to the idea of getting the film crew into the Dome on the Rock. The film then goes on to show them entering the Holy of Holies and praying for Jesus to be at the centre of their lives and the people around them.

God can do the impossible – and as we're led by the Spirit, we can be led into the impossible.

Dancing or Running in the Spirit

The Assemblies of God in America have an explanation of dancing in the Spirit on their website, as they try to explain some of the different manifestations that happen in churches around the world. They claim that these dances are not choreographed and that people tend to dance with their eyes closed as they are led by the Spirit. The website also goes on to note that these people don't tend to bump into other worshippers.[38] I'd probably be a little hesitant to put too many stipulations on what we label as the Holy Spirit, which is why I've also chosen to talk about running in the Spirit here.

From my own personal experience of this sort of thing, I would say that we often get so wrapped up in God that a sense of euphoria sweeps through us and, in our excitement, running or dancing just feels like the natural thing to do. There will always be people that feel that this is their special thing, which it might be. I would love to have people that danced in the Spirit in our church.

Shakes and Making Animal Noises – Toronto Blessing

Of all of the things that have been seen and done in the name of the Spirit, these two are probably the most difficult to understand.

Matthew 28:4 speaks of a physical manifestation of Jesus outside of his tomb. At this point the guards were so afraid that they began to shake, and fell over as if they were asleep. Also the Bible says that the fear of the Lord is the beginning of wisdom and that we have plenty of reason to be afraid of God. As his huge, massive, powerful presence enters our atmosphere, it's not at all illogical to assume that we might be a little scared, and that we may begin to shake.

Personally, I've only had continual shakes once, and that was when I first became a Christian. On that night I asked God to baptise me in his Spirit that I might live a holy life for him. I asked him to take away my sin and all of my addictions – of which one was an addiction to alcohol. I actually fell over in the Spirit that night, even though I didn't believe in that sort of stuff, and as I was laid on the floor I began to shake. When I got up from the floor I kept shaking until long after I got home. I felt hungry, even though I was full, and I felt like something had been taken out of me. Needless to say that my alcoholism was

---

[38] Assemblies of God, *Modern day manifestations of the Spirit*, http://ag.org/top/Beliefs/topics/sptlissues_manifestations.cfm, accessed 26th September 2014.

totally removed. I often say I had no DTs (delirium tremors) but now I look back on it, maybe those shakes were all sorts of addictions, or sins, being removed from me.

As for barking like a dog or making other animal noises, I think that John Arnott's explanation is quite a good one. He claims that a lot of the things that we see during church meetings where the Holy Spirit is present can be put down to a prophetic action. One example of this is a story he tells:

> *Once, at a gathering of pastors in Stirling, Scotland, the worship leader led worship beautifully but every now and again she would crow like a cockerel. When I asked her what was going on, she replied, "I feel like the Lord is saying, 'Church, it's time to wake up! There's a new day coming. It's time to wake up!'"* [39]

At the same time, it is important that these actions do not take the limelight from Jesus.

Floating – New Life Hull

I was watching one of the religious TV channels recently on which a pastor from the New Life church in Hull was speaking. He spoke about 'hosting the presence of God' and told a story of when his dad was the pastor of the church. The story claims that whilst his dad had a guest speaker in, one Sunday, they saw something they had never seen before. There was a common belief that sometimes when an anointed worshipper would begin to worship in Spirit and truth, the Holy Spirit would be attracted to their meeting – after all, the Bible says that God inhabits the praises of his people. So, the old time preacher would often look for the 'anointed worshipper' when things felt a little flat in church. On this particular day the only person that he felt right for the job was a lady that would often 'dance in the Spirit' and so, with a hint of desperation for God's presence, he asked the

---

[39] John Arnott, Revival Magazine, *Manifestations of the Holy Spirit: Responses to some commonly asked questions*, http://revivalmag.com/article/manifestations-holy-spirit-responses-some-commonly-asked-questions, accessed 27th September 2014.

lady to come up to the stage to dance. As she closed her eyes and began to dance around the stage, he did what anyone else would do and closed *his* eyes, for fear that she might fall over or something! Within a few minutes he opened his eyes in fear and shock as the crowd in the hall gasped! The story goes that as she was dancing around the stage with her eyes closed, several people in the congregation had theirs open and, as the Spirit descended into their meeting, something amazing happened. This little old lady who loved to dance in the Spirit danced off the stage and around a fold-back speaker, back onto the stage. She actually floated in mid-air around a speaker in front of hundreds of people. You can see why they had gasped. I would have gasped as she headed towards the edge of the stage, in fear that she was going to fall off, but as she floated a couple of feet off the floor, I guess I probably would have been just a little jealous and worshipful.

God does some amazing things in our stupidity, and we shouldn't feel ashamed to just go for it and see what happens. I previously mentioned the time when I was preaching at the church in Worcester[40] and was determined to try a technique that we see on TV quite a lot, despite the fact that most Christians and pastors would say that my talk had no depth or substance. I felt that God was encouraging me to be outrageously different and that he didn't want me to succumb to the pressure of looking and sounding 'right' on the pulpit. As I preached a simple message that was leading up to an altar-call, I began to get nervous at the prospect of actually calling people to the front for the baptism in the Spirit, just in case Bonnke's results were down to his fame and not his technique, anointing or what the Spirit was doing. As I made the call, a crowd of people came to the front, and all of a sudden I plucked up the courage to be totally and outrageously Pentecostal. After praying for all of the people that came forward that evening, I decided I was going to try prophesying over the ones who had stayed in their seats. I began to go around the church praying for people one by one. There were some amazing things that happened that evening as I pushed the boat out and felt a little silly. One man, the next week, came to me before the church

---

[40] See page 22.

service and asked for a chat in private. He explained to me that he had watched some Christian TV and hadn't believed that a lot of the stuff was true – like the prophetic and healing. He asked me if I had been speaking to his wife, or secretly following him around, because when had I prayed for him I mentioned financial difficulty and the struggles that he was facing at home. As I prayed he felt that God was speaking to him, counselling him and ministering to him through the prophetic – but it didn't fit his theology or his previous experience.

In my stupidity God had done something amazing, not just for that man, but for many other people that day too. Maybe we should be less bothered about what we think we look like, and more bothered about giving room for the Holy Spirit to do his job in our churches.

Freakish Weather – Elim Bible Week, R. T. Kendall

It was the Easter break of 2012, and near two thousand people had crammed into the Telford International Centre for Elim's national conference. R. T. Kendall had taken the pulpit as hundreds of people waited expectantly for him to preach. He chose to preach the gospel and challenge ministers in our movement to do the same. As his talk neared an end you could feel God in the atmosphere, and as an onlooker I personally felt in awe of God, a lot like when I had first met Jesus, just wowed by his presence. Just as the hammer came down on his preach, rain started smashing on top of the tin roof, like a roar from above. The same sort of thing has happened in our church too – almost as if the weather is confirming you're in line with God, like the very voice of the preacher got the weather excited.

It reminds me of a time I was watching the television a few years back and a presenter was telling the story of a small town in Alaska that was plagued by alcoholism and suicide for decades. As people turned up to worship God one day, a rushing wind blew through the city and through the building that they were in. In this small town they saw a revival as people were set free from addiction and everyone began to worship God.

I believe that worship is key to hosting God's presence. The Bible says that God inhabits the praises of his people, and there have been no greater times of presence than when I've been wrapped up in worship for God. On one occasion when I had recently become a

Christian, I started worshipping God via YouTube in the evening and got carried away! I must have been driving my neighbours mad as I shouted like a football hooligan, singing songs to God until 3am. When I couldn't sing anymore I started shouting in tongues. Luckily my wife and children were used to me being loud until the early hours, but my Muslim neighbours must have been livid. The power of God in my life was epic though. I walked on clouds for months until I was told to get it together by my pastor!

You can begin to praise God by simply telling him, and yourself, who he is: why he's famous and why he's awesome! It's okay to get carried away.

4

Why We Need Him

At the beginning of this book you may have asked yourself, "What's the big deal?" or, "Why do we need a relationship with the Holy Spirit?" I would hope that by now you might be thinking more along the lines of, "Wow! This sounds awesome! I've been missing out on so much; how do I get started?" We'll get to that soon. First, I want to give you a few more reasons to want him. As we enter a new chapter on the subject of why we need the Holy Spirit, I'm anticipating the moment when we can start the journey with him. My hope would be that this chapter would only breed a deeper longing for his presence.

So, now we're going to look at some experiences of famous people from the past, and maybe a couple of my own, in an attempt to understand why we need him.

Holiness

The Bible is quite clear in instructing us to be holy,[41] and teaches us that our minds have to be be renewed, but these words – 'holy' or 'renewed' – can only be accomplished if we know what they mean. Remember that the word 'holy' means 'to be set apart'. God says that

---

[41] e.g. John 8:11; Matthew 5:48; 1 Peter 1:16.

his ways are higher than ours, that his mind works on a different level to ours, and this is what makes him holy.

I've separated the concepts of holiness and sanctification in this chapter. This is because holiness doesn't necessarily mean keeping laws or acting in a particular way; instead it speaks of bringing your ambitions, thoughts, soul and mind into alignment with God's. Both John Wesley and Charles Finney – well-known Christians from church history – claim that the essence of holiness is to fully sacrifice your whole self to God; bringing your heart and will – by which they mean your ambitions and dreams – before God and surrendering them before him.[42] To be holy is to have your mind renewed by the very fact that your utmost desire is to come in line with what God is thinking on any and every issue. This is truly dying to your own selfish ambition or drive for success. When you think as God does, your lifestyle and the choices that you make – how you treat people, or even think about them – will become like those of God. Living a life of grace becomes natural, and only seeing the positive in people becomes an easy exercise.

However, this can only be done with the help and guidance of the Holy Spirit. A holy lifestyle can only be accomplished by walking in step with him every minute of every day. It comes from allowing the Holy Spirit in you to renew your mind on a daily basis, asking him to change your worldview and your core beliefs.[43] My wife has been studying psychology since we've been living in Lincoln, and I find it fascinating how God is constantly using scientific concepts to show me the truths of his scripture and the depths of his ways – that is, his thoughts and motives. Lately Laura has come across the concept of cognitive dissonance, which describes how humans struggle to behave contrary to their core beliefs. So, if you believe that it is impossible to live life without breaking one of God's very few commandments for Gentile believers – like eating food sacrificed to

---

[42] L. G. Parkhurst Jr, *Charles Finney: Principles of Holiness*, (Minneapolis: Bethany House Publishers, 1984), 94-95; H. C. Backhouse, *John Wesley: A plain man's guide to holiness*, (London: Hodder & Stoughton Limited, 1988), 15-17.

[43] J. Cooper, *Cognitive Dissonance: Fifty years of a classic theory*, (London: SAGE Publications Ltd, 2007), 6-10.

idols and sexual immorality[44] – then you will naturally find it easy to break those rules as your core belief is that you'll fail in the pursuit of holiness. However, if you ask the Holy Spirit to renew your mind and alter your core belief then you may come to a place where your core belief is that of God himself: "I am set apart!" "My ways are higher than the world around me that has held me captive for so long." "My life belongs to Jesus, and so do my thoughts and my ambitions!" Thus you will begin to act selflessly, always in tune with how God is thinking; never even thinking about sin, or rules, or self-promotion. This is true holiness, and it can only be achieved with the help and guidance of the Holy Spirit. Holiness, then, is the redemption of your way of thinking and your core beliefs or values.

To bring some more light to this, let me tell you a story of a lady in our church who, for many years, was like anyone else when it came to relationships with the opposite sex – she struggled with sex outside of marriage. This particular lady came to faith in our church, and entered a love relationship with Jesus in a special way. There were a few times that we prayed for her to become more holy and to be baptised in the Spirit of Jesus, and believed that he had answered our prayers. However, one day she came to our church leaders extremely worried and in despair. That week she had slept with a man outside of marriage and she couldn't console herself. She made a statement that day that it would never happen again. She is worthy, not worthless. She is a member of the royal family in heaven, and her thoughts are higher than they were before. Her ways are higher than they were before. I believe that her core values and beliefs have changed under the power and guidance of the Holy Spirit, and now she finds it impossible to do the things that she once wanted to do.

1 John 1 says:

> *God is light; in him there is no darkness at all. If we claim to have fellowship with him yet walk in the darkness, we lie and do not live by the truth. But if we walk in the light, as he is in the light, we have fellowship with one another, and the blood of Jesus, his Son, purifies us from all sin.*

---

[44] Acts 15:20.

Sanctification

I love that the Holy Spirit is well known for the power that he brings to believers, but I think much the same as Smith Wigglesworth did in his day. Smith Wigglesworth is possibly the most well-known healing evangelist the world has seen, and the healing power shown in his ministry was amazing. However, it's a little known fact that for Wigglesworth "faith, purity and power were inextricably linked".[45]

According to Baker's Evangelical Dictionary, sanctification is primarily linked with function, or the action associated with which a thing – or, in our case, person – was made for.[46] So sanctification isn't the same as holiness. If holiness is being set apart in the way you think, then sanctification is being set apart in the way that you behave. This is highlighted by what Polly Wigglesworth, Smith's wife, said after he was baptised in the Spirit:

> I never saw such a change... I have never been able to cook anything since that time that has not pleased him. Nothing too hot or cold, everything is just right.[47]

As we get closer to the Holy Spirit, his work in us is shown through our relationships with other people in our lives. We begin to act like Jesus. Sanctification, then, is the practical outworking of being Christ-like. As believers we are able to become more stable in our emotions meaning that we become harder to upset. When someone is overly critical towards me, I act gracefully – I don't take offence, even if they mean to be offensive. I just love them like Jesus does.

With both holiness and sanctification, the old saying 'Practice makes perfect' is very true. You make it your priority to be holy and sanctified in every situation, and if you fail, you apologise and keep on trying. The further you go along the journey of holiness and sanctification, the easier it gets for you to be Christ-like. However, if you start making excuses to be rude, abusive or arrogant then you

---

[45] J. Wilson, *Wigglesworth: the complete story*, (Milton Keynes: Authentic Media, 2002), 84.
[46] BibleStudyTools.com, *Sanctification*, http://www.biblestudytools.com/dictionaries/bakers-evangelical-dictionary/sanctification.html, accessed 17th October 2014.
[47] Wilson, *Wigglesworth*, 30.

will fall into a trap that halts your progress. Some people feel that their testimony needs to be maintained by acting aggressively towards people, but Jesus was meek. Like an iron hand in a velvet glove. There's no such thing as a rough Christian, and so we need to drop the 'top boy' attitude to become Christ-like for the sake of God's testimony in us.

It is totally possible to decide, on the day that you receive the Spirit of God, to say no to sin and living for yourself, to become more like Jesus without ever turning back from that. You just make the commitment and then stick by it.

Power

It would be a crime to mention Smith Wigglesworth without mentioning the power of the Holy Spirit. During the early 20th Century the UK was overrun with an exciting revival that spread across the nation, and this was largely due to the power of the Spirit. Wigglesworth and George Jeffreys, another healing evangelist, were two of the most well-known preachers of their time. The story goes that Wigglesworth's death came about due to the shock of one of his prayers not being answered. They say that one in ten people that he prayed for were healed, and Jeffreys is believed to have been even more successful, with one in seven people that he prayed for being healed.[48]

The Bible says that the same power that raised Christ from the dead lives in us – his followers.

Since being a Christian, I've seen some amazing things happen – before, during, and after Bible college. One day I was preaching at a small church in Evesham – telling everyone about my vision for Chav Church, and sharing my story of salvation. The evening before I was asking God for an amazing word of prophecy to really glorify him,

---

[48] T. Walsh, *History of Healing*, Lecture, Regents Theological College, West Malvern, Worcestershire, February 2012. At Regents we had the luxury of spending time with people that had actually been present during the ministry years of these two heroes of the faith. If you're ever looking to raise your faith levels I would recommend reading some old magazines from the turn of the 20th Century. Something like The Evangel or Confidence.

when I heard the name 'James'. James just happens to be one of my favourite books of the Bible so I thought he wanted me to read from it. As I started to read the book, I felt God uttered the name 'James' to me again. I then realised that he wanted me to call out or pray for someone called James. That's quite a risk as there are so many names and not many people. It's not like standing in church and asking people with back pain to come forward. I told God that I would only say the name when I felt his push – almost like a nervous or sick sort of feeling. Whilst speaking I told everyone that I was going to pray for the sick and prophesy over people, and that they needed to come forward for prayer at the end of my talk if they wanted to receive a blessing from God. Lots of people came forward at the end and I prayed for healing for many people, and prophesied over a few too. One lady came forward and asked me to prophesy. This was the first person that had actually asked for a prophecy. I felt that sick, nervous feeling in my stomach and asked her if she knew someone called James. She said yes, in shock. It was her brother, and so we prayed for him.[49] I carried on and told her that she had a pain in her stomach. I believed this was the case because I felt a specific pain in my own stomach. She started to cry, which is when God said that the pain was caused by anxiety. I told her that God knew that she was afraid of being in her own home and that he wanted her to know that he was her protector. She fell down to her knees and began to worship him.

The power of God will only be seen in your life when you step out and take a risk. He will only heal people through your hands if you put your hands on people for healing. He will only speak through you if you open your mouth. Since I've started praying for healing through the laying on of hands, I've seen cancer healed in two people. You must step out in faith if you're going to see the power of God released in your life.

---

[49] I think that in this case the name was just God's way of letting the lady know that he knew her and wanted to meet with her. I never found out what happened with her brother. We just prayed for his salvation.

Comfort

I once went to a men's conference in Birmingham where there was a guest speaker by the name of Mark Stibbe – author of 'I Am Your Father'[50]. As Stibbe began to preach you could almost feel the Holy Spirit stirring among the eight hundred men in the room. At the end of the service there was an amazing moment which, for all of those there, will be engraved on our souls, as the preacher began to explain that whilst we find it easy to forgive others as men, we find it almost impossible to forgive ourselves. I had my eyes closed as the Spirit of Jesus began to cause hundreds of grown men to cry. I don't think I'd be lying if I said there was barely a dry eye in that room.

The Holy Spirit, for those eight hundred men, became their close, familiar friend who came to their side to help them in a difficult place.

Worship

Some of my most meaningful times of worship have been when a hush falls over a meeting and the Holy Spirit begins to cause his followers to worship in spirit and truth. Myles Munroe, author and world renowned minister, states that the Greek word used for worship literally means 'to kiss' – just as a dog might lick his master's hand. This is a very intimate and humble expression of the word; to lower yourself to that position, almost begging for your master's attention and love. Coincidentally, the beginning of the Greek word, *pros-,* means to be near or beside, which could lead us into thinking that with our Paraclete beside us, we're able to move close enough to our Master, approaching him as we would do with royalty, to bow down before him and kiss his hand.[51] It just so happens that when we come before royalty, or majesty, it is often the case that we become somewhat more dignified. While we may shout and scream from a distance, when we enter into his presence in spirit and truth, dignity and reverence are often our form of worship.

Just recently I was worshipping alongside fifteen hundred men at XCEL Men's Conference at Life Church in Bradford, where there was

---

[50] 2010, ISBN: 1854249371

[51] M. Munroe, *The Glory of Living: Keys to releasing your personal glory,* (Shippensburg: Destiny Image Publishers Inc., 2005), 109-110.

a definite sense that the Spirit of God was present in a special way. As silence grew over the hundreds of men, people began to experience God in new ways. Some men were healed from emotional issues, some from physical, and up to two hundred were so overwhelmed by his presence that they committed to follow Jesus for the first time. As an altar-call for salvation rang out at the end of that awesome time, hundreds of men streamed out to be saved. It was amazing.

I want to be like Obed-Edom[52] who, after experiencing the presence of God, decided to leave his life and wealth behind to follow it for the rest of his life.

Wisdom

I was chatting to Stuart Bell, a church leader in Alive Church Lincoln and the Ground Level Network, in a prayer meeting that involved some church leaders from our city. As Stuart was talking he mentioned the way that as you get further along in your walk with the Holy Spirit his thoughts and wisdom begin to become your own. It's as though you align your thoughts, motives and actions with his. This means that everyday tasks become God-inspired.

An example of this is a radio interview I had with a presenter who was renowned for being a little 'out of order'. The whole time I was praying that he wouldn't ask me a controversial question, but as he questioned me, I was almost surprised at the stuff that was coming out of my own mouth. I even managed to sneak in the gospel during the interview about Chav Church. As my friends and family listened in, my biggest critics (my wife and I) were pleasantly surprised that I didn't ruin my ministry with a crazy statement. But the wisdom came from the Holy Spirit.

---

[52] 2 Samuel 6 onwards.

5

Beginning Your Journey

I remember sitting at the front of the Fire Conference in Birmingham whilst Reinhard Bonnke preached on reckless faith. All I wanted to do was to jump up on the stage and ask him to pray for my faith. There was a stirring within me and my heart began to beat faster.

Perhaps, like me, you feel like that now. As I imagine the opportunity that is ahead of me to experience the power, love, and grace of the Spirit of God, I have that same sense of "I can't wait any longer!"

So here we go!

There are a number of ways to start this journey. In this chapter we'll look at a few of them and hopefully get the chance to practise them whilst going through these pages.

The Bible speaks about being baptised in the Spirit of God. The original meaning of the word baptism is 'to be saturated'. If we imagine that water represents the Holy Spirit of God (which is biblical, by the way) and that we are like a sponge, then to be baptised in God's Spirit would be like us being plunged into the Spirit, having him saturate us – soaking us through.

This means that if we are to be truly saturated in the Holy Spirit, we'll need to get into a place where the atmosphere is brimming with his presence. This could be a prayer meeting, a church service, or even in private devotions that are God led and filled.

Another thing about this analogy is that it lends itself to the idea of the world around you and the troubles that you go through being like a hand that squeezes your sponge. The Bible tells us to keep being filled with the Spirit of God, however there is only one baptism. If you enter into his presence often enough then you should stay saturated to the core, but you may feel the need to be dipped into his presence frequently as you are squeezed out in the world.

So, how do we get saturated?

Pray by Yourself

The Bible speaks about how the disciples of Jesus were waiting in a room together, praying for the Holy Spirit of God. I would liken this to a prayer meeting with some friends.

As they were waiting for the Comforter to come, there was a rushing wind and the Spirit entered the room appearing as a flame flickering like a tongue. The flame then split between them and came to rest on each of the disciples. It seemed that they must have felt incredibly energetic, and suddenly they were in the street, speaking in foreign languages and performing miracles.

My wife, Laura, was baptised in a similar way. One night when she was putting our daughter to bed she began to pray out to God. She claims that at that moment she began to speak in a language that she didn't know. Most Pentecostals and Charismatic Christians would call this speaking in tongues. This was Laura's first experience of this new experiential faith.

Some pastors tell me that in recent times they have encouraged their church to pray for the baptism in the Spirit in private at home.

Getting Hands On

Throughout the New Testament we see Jesus and the Apostles touching people to bring healing, and to baptise them in the Spirit of God. This is my preferred method when it comes to praying for the baptism because there's a hint of intimacy attached to it.

The Jews in Jesus' time believed that only God himself would touch people for healing. They drew a picture that showed all of the prophets of God asking him to stretch out his hand, but they would never stretch out their hands themselves. In the New Testament we see Jesus stretching his hand out to touch his people, showing that he had God's authority and power. He then sent his disciples into the world, telling them to do the same. This means that we, as his disciples, have the power and authority to do what he did on this earth.

John the Baptist told his followers that Jesus would come and baptise people in the Spirit and in fire. As Jesus left the earth to be with his Father in heaven, he gave us the authority to baptise people in the Spirit of God.

Personally, if I was to have someone put their hands on me so that I could be filled with the Spirit, I would need to know that they were also filled with the Spirit. For this reason, I would look at their lifestyle before asking them to pray for me. The guy that laid his hands on me for the baptism in the Spirit is a veteran minister that, I know from his close friends and family, gets up at 6am each morning to pray for a couple of hours before starting his day. He whole life is devoted to Jesus, and his lifestyle says that Jesus is Lord. Make sure you find someone that you trust to lay their hands on you for this amazing, intimate gift.

The Breath of God

It's not often that I've seen this particular method being used in the Bible, or in church life, but nonetheless it can be found in both.

Before Jesus went to heaven, after his resurrection, he breathed on his disciples and told them to receive the Spirit of God. There doesn't seem to be any physical manifestation that takes place on this occasion, but I'm sure he wouldn't have done it if there was nothing happening in the spiritual realm.

At this point, the disciples had already been performing miracles in the name of Jesus and had been preaching across Israel. They had already witnessed and believed the death and resurrection of Jesus, and they had made him Lord of their lives when they began to follow him. So this baptism came after their salvation. Yet there was another moment coming, in Acts chapter 2, where they would receive the Spirit once again.

I once heard a preacher say that Jesus had to die for his Spirit to be released upon all men because until that point the Spirit would merely rest on certain men for a specific amount of time. This action could well be the time that Joel's prophecy came to fruition.[53]

In terms of modern day examples of this action, I've only ever seen it happen on television. I've felt prompted to breathe on people so that they can receive the Spirit of God in my own ministry, though. I'm sure that this is practised regularly in Spirit-filled churches but maybe just not as regularly as laying hands on people.

During Water Baptism

Some people are baptised in the Holy Spirit during their baptism in water. I've heard of people speaking about how the water had a different texture to it, like it was oily or something, and how they received a vision whilst being baptised. It's not mentioned in the Bible as a method of being saturated in the Spirit of God but, like I mentioned before, there are ways that God interacts with us that are not mentioned in scripture. In fact, the Apostle John said in his Gospel that there wasn't enough paper available to write of all the things that Jesus did.

All I would say is that if you eagerly desire an intimate relationship with God, he will meet with you when the time is right. You'll know that you've been saturated when you begin to exhibit spiritual behaviours.

During a Worship Service

It could be the case that as you worship God in a church setting, you receive the baptism. Again, I've heard about this happening but it's not mentioned in the Bible.

One lady tells her story online:

I had a friend that went to holiness meetings and she talked me into going one night. There was something there.

I had never seen such happy people in all my life, and I was so miserable. I wanted to feel what they were feeling. I

---

[53] Joel 2:28.

started seeking for the Holy Ghost because I liked what I saw.

She continues talking about the moment that she finally received the Spirit's baptism:

I said, "God I cannot live without the Holy Ghost, I've got to have this Holy Ghost, that's all there is to it. I just have to have it." I received stammering lips from day one, but it took me a while to understand that this was the Holy Ghost.

It was like a bolt of lightning came down, struck me in my left leg, lifted my leg up and took me out into the aisle.[54]

The lady then goes on to talk about how the Holy Spirit interacted with her after that worship service.

Whichever way you are a baptised in the Spirit of God, it's important to note that being saturated in his Spirit is not a euphoric moment as you sing the song you like, it is a life-changing God experience that moves you to become more like Jesus, both in behaviour and character.

My prayer went something along the lines of, "God, I'm so desperate to get close to you, and to know you. I'm scared that by my own efforts I won't be able to meet the demand of making you Lord of my life. Please fill me with your Holy Spirit, baptise me, saturate me so that I can live a life that is pleasing to you! Amen."

Power from Heaven

Wow! So I'm excited and maybe a little bit nervous with anticipation after praying a prayer that essentially asks God to make me like Jesus. I have a picture in my mind of Emperor Palpatine from Star Wars; that moment when he kills Mace Windu and lightning bolts come out of his hand as he screeches, "UNLIMITED POWER!" You know that if you have been baptised in the Spirit of God, the Bible

---

[54] Isaiah 58's Free Gospel Resources, *How We Receive The Holy Ghost Baptism*, http://www.isaiah58.com/holyghostbaptism.html, accessed 3rd January 2015.

Getting to Know the Holy Spirit

says that you have the same power in you that raised Jesus from the dead.

6

Supernatural Gifts

The Bible gives a long list of things that the Holy Spirit can give you supernatural power for, that are called "gifts of the Spirit". These include all sorts of things, from healing to the supernatural gift of administration. In order to not get too carried away, we'll just look at those gifts that are in the Bible and try to explain some of them quite briefly.

Romans 12

GIVING

Giving is something that we are all encouraged to do in the Bible, but the supernatural giver is something special. These people often give double or treble their tithe, and God quite often, knowing that they'll carry on giving, puts them into a position of giving more. We all hear stories of preachers that have given cars away and then received something special from God. I once heard of a man that gave something away and then was given a jet. Personally I don't even think I could afford the fuel for a jet, let alone the insurance or a pilot.

I've found that those with the supernatural gift of giving seem to be quite wise in finding a decent job. These guys are often blessed in business because God has gifted them to the church to give all they have. Some might even give up to 50% of their income to the church to help with the church's mission.

If you have this gift you should train it by giving more generously to a single entity, and by giving outside of yourself. It's easy to give a large amount of money when you have huge amounts spare, but Jesus commended the woman who gave her only two coins above the man that gave his 10%, despite the 10% probably being a larger sum of money. Also, let me encourage you to go for that promotion. God might well give it to you so that you can bless his church; after all, you are his gift to the church.

LEADERSHIP

Every now and again you find someone in church that people just seem to follow. Recently we had a guy commit his life to Jesus and within a few months other people in our church were openly willing to follow his leadership. In our church we have an annual awards ceremony, where we have a few awards that each person in church can nominate someone to win. On this particular occasion, despite there being more seasoned and mature Christians available to win, the person that overwhelmingly won our Emerging Leader Award was a guy that had been a Christian for barely a few months.

In truth, authority is not something that you take, authority is given and it must be given by God and those who follow your leadership. If you have to ask or fight to be the boss, the chances are that you're not worthy of the job.

If you have the Holy Spirit gift of leadership, you should concentrate on your character in order to train your gift. Leaders should lead by example. A leader will lead by walking in a particular way as his followers mimic him, whereas a butcher will whip his sheep from behind to force them into a pen or abattoir.

Bill Hybels has written a great book called 'Courageous Leadership'. I would point you in that direction to get you started.

MERCY

A dictionary definition of this word is 'to show compassion or forgiveness towards someone who deserves punishment'. Christian

Schwarz, a writer from the United States, claims that this gift is particularly an *action* gift.[55] I would describe it as being able to act with compassion towards someone who continues to get themselves into difficult situations despite knowing that they could, and possibly should, help themselves but choose not to.

It's like seeing a homeless man at the side of the street who chooses to buy a scratch card with his benefits instead of buying food or lodging. Instead of trying to give this man advice or complaining about how he chooses to use his money, someone with the supernatural gift of mercy will almost blindly choose to relieve his suffering.

The gift of mercy and the gift of grace are intrinsically linked, as you can't show mercy without having a certain amount of grace. Training this gift is more about using it regularly than reading about it. The more you just give yourself away to people that need your mercy, the better you'll get at seeing past the circumstance to minister to the person.

PROPHECY

Prophecy is one of the gifts that it used quite regularly in church services and in everyday life. Sometimes we even prophesy without knowing it. Prophecy is the act of speaking on behalf of God. It could be that you feel a certain way emotionally or that you have an inner sense that you need to say a certain thing. In my own experience it has usually been the case that I feel very strongly about saying something; I almost always feel an emotional disturbance when God wants me to speak.

It's important that when prophesying you do it with a certain amount of sensitivity. For example, I very rarely say things like, "God says…" or, "I think the Lord is saying…" This is because there's a chance that you can mistake your own emotions for what God is actually saying. We've all heard stories of times when 'prophets' have told brother and sister that they'll have a beautiful family together one

---

[55] C. A. Schwarz, *The 3 Colors of Ministry: A trinitarian approach to identifying and developing your spiritual gifts,* (Illinois: ChurchSmart Resources, 2001), 108.

day! RT Kendall, a well known writer and preacher, says that often when people say that God is speaking through them, they are name-dropping to add credibility to what they are saying.[56] If God is really speaking through you, you won't need to let everyone know before you say something. Everyone will recognize when God's words challenge their lives.

The best way to train this gift is to be faithful to it. If you feel God is saying something, find a way to get it out. This could be done by praying into what you feel God is saying, or by finding a way to bring the words into a conversation. If you are trusted by your pastor, and you don't try to prophesy every week, they may let you speak on God's behalf in your church service. I tend to sit close to the front in church so that if I feel this way inclined I can whisper in the ear of my pastor's or elders' ears. You will learn to distinguish God's voice the more that you practise this gift.

SERVICE

It often seems that only 10% of the church do 90% of the work. However, 'service' is listed as a Holy Spirit gift by the apostle Paul. In the same way that Schwarz and his team have found that only 13% of the church have the spiritual gift of mercy,[57] it's quite normal that only 10% of the church will have the gift of service. If this is the case then we should release the servants in our churches as we would a prophet or teacher, and shouldn't expect everyone to minister to God with this particular gift, just as we wouldn't expect everyone to speak in tongues.

Serving, then, is the supernatural motivation to get involved with the nitty-gritty of church. A decent servant will be willing to clean toilets, sweep floors, or set up sound systems. What's more, they enjoy doing it so much that they turn up early every week so that they can do more. Oh, how the church needs more servants to be set free into their ministry! If you're a servant, tell your pastor that you think

---

[56] R. T. Kendall, *Holy Fire: A balanced, biblical look at the Holy Spirit's work in our lives,* (Lake Mary: Charisma House Book Group, 2014), 150-151.
[57] Schwarz, *3 Colors*, 108.

you have this awesome gift, and ask him/her if you can get involved with anything.

TEACHING

The teaching gift is one of the main gifts that is taught, gleaned and encouraged in our churches today. Many people, when looking for a new church, try to find one where they can receive "good teaching". This in turn places a high value on the gift, so a lot of people try hard to train themselves in it – and some people want the gift even though they do not yet have it.

Being a good teacher isn't just about speaking spiritual truths and deep concepts from the pulpit. It's actually more about making those truths and concepts easy to understand for the listeners. The Holy Spirit teacher is able to take thirty years of study and experience to a group of novices and children and make them understand it. One of the best people I've ever heard doing this is one of my old lecturers, Keith Warrington.

If you are going to train this gift, you will need to get learning. It is impossible to teach something that you haven't already learnt. Get your head into decent books written by trusted authors.

GRACE

Grace is different from forgiveness, although they are linked and the two are often confused. If forgiveness is giving someone a free pass on something that they've done wrong to you, then grace is not taking offence when someone does something that could upset you. The beauty of Jesus' grace for us is that he chose not to take offence at our sin despite the fact that it was all in the future when he died.

As an example, if a person accidentally bumps your car in the car park, you have the choice to take offence, which might include scrutinising their driving and being angry with them, or not to take offence. Not to take offence would be to affirm that person and encourage them. Maybe if they are part of your church, you might embrace them in a hug in order to relieve their stress and let them know that you have chosen not to take offence.

However, a bump in the car is slightly different to a member of your family 'slagging you off' to your friends. It's at these times that you strengthen and train the Holy Spirit gift of grace.

ENCOURAGEMENT

Often in ministry I find that people like to compliment my preaching, writing or actions. Sometimes it feels as though people are trying to tickle my ears, and similarly it can feel like the preachers of this world are trying to tickle the ears of those that are listening, by preaching the things that they want to hear. However, every now and again I come across a Barnabas.

Acts 4:36 says that the meaning of the name Barnabas is "Son of Encouragement", and in Romans 6 encouragement is listed as one of the gifts of the Spirit. Now and then we see a supernatural gift of encouragement in someone's life. This isn't the ability just to be an encouragement when they choose, but it is a default spirit of encouragement that they carry at all times.

These people will barely ever know what they bring to the church when they enter a room, but when you're feeling rough, a simple rub on the shoulder or an embrace from a Son of Encouragement can put your world back together.

It is no surprise then that the Apostle Paul needed Barnabas on his travels. Ground-breaking Christians, or pioneers, are often discouraged by those that like their comfort zones. I can imagine that Barnabas was the driving force behind a lot of what Paul did in his early ministry. Sometimes as pioneers we need a Barnabas to pull the knives out of our backs and lick the wounds of a pioneer ministry.

We should all try to be encouraging, as Spirit-filled Christians, but these guys have a special ability to be able to do it without even trying. If you have this gift, you can train yourself to use it more effectively by using all forms of communication – like touch, body language, and even writing letters. A handwritten letter from an encourager is priceless.

1 Corinthians 12

ADMINISTRATION

John Stott, possibly one of the greatest Bible teachers of recent times, notes that when people think of charisma and power they often think of people with spectacular personalities, but they forget that administration is also listed as one of the supernatural gifts that God has given to his church.[58]

The church needs people that like to do things properly, efficiently and correctly, especially in the current financial climate. Did you know that if the registrar at your wedding gets a detail wrong, you're not legally married? I'm sure you can imagine how dreadful it would be if you had stayed pure for your whole life, waiting for your wedding day, only to find out that when you finally consummated your marriage, you were not actually married.

The church needs people that love details and instruction booklets. If this is your gift, you should never be ashamed that you take longer to make decisions, and you should make sure that no-one dismisses your beautiful, powerful gift.

Jobs that you might be good at in church include Finance Officer, Registrar and Administrator.

APOSTLE

According to Strong's Concordance, the word 'apostle' means 'a messenger' or 'a delegate'.[59] Some of the words used to describe apostles in the New Testament focus more on the sender of the messenger, or the master of the delegate, which points to the fact that these were messenger or delegates of Jesus.

If we look at how they worked in the New Testament and how they work in today's church, we can see two distinct characteristics:

- *They are pioneers.* This means that they will start new ministries and go to new places. In the New Testament you will

---

[58] J. Stott, *Baptism and Fullness*, (Illinois: Inter-Varsity Press, 2007), 133.
[59] Bible Hub, *Apostolos*, http://biblehub.com/greek/652.htm, accessed 19th January 2015.

find that they tend to take the gospel to unreached areas of the world.

- *They are respected leaders in the church* who are given authority to speak into the leadership and spirit of a host of churches that they may even be seen as governing. Take, for example, some of the people that would spearhead a denomination or be asked to give guidance to a group of churches about discipleship or evangelism. The apostle is given a special ability to bring guidance in the wider church.

Note: if you find yourself inclined to go from church to church and point out the mistakes of the pastors, that does not mean you are a prophet or apostle. In this case, it is usual a signal that you need some healing. I encourage you to commit yourself to a church where you can be reconciled, redeemed and restored to a right relationship with those around you. Then God will begin to use you in a right way, for the building up of his church.

An apostle is given authority by God that is recognised by the wider church.

Discernment

Discernment has to be the best gift for any budding leader in the church. The Bible says to eagerly seek the better gifts, and it names prophecy in particular, but I think the best gift when it comes to leadership has to be discernment.

This spiritual gift helps you to distinguish between motives. Sometimes people will stand up and prophesy in church because they want to be noticed, when they should in fact be using that specific Holy Spirit gift to increase the faith in the church. Sometimes people will give advice based on what's best for them, instead of what's best for the person that they are advising.

If we should seek the gift of prophecy for the sake of building the church, then maybe we should also seek the gift of discernment for the sake of church governance.

This gift can also help to appropriately deal with the actions of people that roll about on the floor, or claim to have psychological issues. In some churches psychological issues have been blamed on the demonic, when in reality there is some physical damage to a person's brain. This does not glorify God in any way and is damaging to the faith of onlookers. However, sometimes things that we might normally attest to the Holy Spirit can actually be put down to our human frailties or the enemy.

My general take on this is, if someone's actions are drawing the attention away from what God is doing in a meeting, then that person may well be acting under the jurisdiction of the demonic. However, sometimes you may need to keep this information to yourself until the right time comes for you to confront the situation or person. This again requires discernment – when to act and when not to. You can see why this is a valuable gift for any leader.

FAITH

I had only been a Christian for about a month when I was cautioned by some people concerning 'faith healing'. However, before criticising another's view on faith, it is important that we have a clear understanding of what it actually is. Unfortunately, this book doesn't allow me the space to indulge the hidden recesses of the doctrine of faith, but I'll try to explain a little about what it means for the man that has this gift and how to train it.

To have faith does not mean to have faith in one's self, or to have faith in faith itself. Instead it means to have faith in God. If you find that it is very easy for you to believe that God can do anything, that he will do whatever you ask of him, and that it is even possible for him to create the universe with words, then you probably have the gift of faith to some degree.

Your faith will begin to grow when you ask God to do the increasingly impossible things in ministry and life that can't otherwise be done. As you ask God for these things, your faith will begin to grow, and you'll begin to see faith through new eyes.

It has gotten to the point in my own walk where I actually believe that God has given me an anointing to lead people to Jesus, and to heal very serious diseases in his name. I believe that most of the words that exit my mouth are God's words, and I actually believe that if you put your total trust in God and die fully to yourself, you can live a life with no sin in it whatsoever. From speaking to other Christians I know that this can be the case across the board and the reality for every believer.

With all of this in mind, the way in which I pray and act begins to change, which in turn makes my faith grow ever stronger.

In the beginning I had very little faith in my prayers being answered and so I would recite what I call 'fake prayers'. These are prayers that you say because you need to, but don't have faith for. Inside they feel like just a normal sentence aimed at God, but you're not really speaking to him, you're speaking to the person you're praying for. As time goes on, however, you start to pray prayers that you actually believe. It's like a feeling deep inside that says, "God is actually going to hear this prayer and answer immediately!" Let's call these prayers 'faith-filled prayers'. As you begin to pray more 'faith-filled prayers' you'll find that they get answered, and eventually your faith begins to grow. Soon you get to the place in which you notice God is even answering the prayers you don't really have faith for, and so your faith moves to a higher level.

Faith isn't just believing in God. The book of James says that even the demons believe in Jesus and shudder. Faith is taking action on what you believe. Believing a bridge can hold your weight is not faith; walking on it is.

HEALING

I spent a lot of time in Bible College researching healing and how it works. If you get really deep into the books, you'll find that no-one really fully understands the gift. Some believe that the gift is given to the receiver instead of the minister; so many people will be given a gift of healing, but no-one is a healer. In practice, however, I've found it to be slightly different. Heidi Baker, a well known minister who pioneers new churches in Mozambique, will often call all of the deaf people out from a crowd when she is speaking. She obviously finds that when she prays for deaf people she has more success than when she prays for those with other illnesses. Reinhard Bonnke, another really well known preacher, tends to call blind people out of the crowd first. I heard him say once that he feels that he has more success with the blind being healed at his meetings. I personally have found that when I pray for people with cancer, I have more faith than what I would if I prayed for a deaf or blind person. This could lend itself to the notion that God gives different people a certain level of faith for healing a particular illness.

The other thing that I've noticed in ministry is that sometimes there's a special moment when heaven meets earth, when our prayer, "Let your kingdom come on earth as it is in heaven!" is actually answered, and in that moment amazing miracles take place. These times can extend beyond an hour, or even a day, into months or years.

In whatever format you find your faith rising, and success occurring, in administering healing the main thing is to keep on doing it. Don't get too worried about repeating prayers or getting into a habit of praying a certain thing over and over. I've prayed for so many people to be healed that I've run out of original prayers and so I just pray whatever feels right at the time. It could even be the same prayer for ten people in a line, but luckily it's not about my words, it's about God's kingdom and his glory!

HELPS

In 1 Corinthians 12 the gift of being able to help others is mentioned. It would be easy to confuse this gift with that of serving, or with mercy, but in fact it is quite different.

If serving is the supernatural motivation to get on with the nitty-gritty of life – serving God by doing seemingly menial but nonetheless important tasks, like getting the chairs ready for church – then helps looks more like driving your pastor to a preaching engagement so that he has an hour spare to go through his sermon.

Helps is less about serving the big picture and more about removing a time-consuming task from the person that you're helping. For me, when I was back in Northampton I felt it my 'job' to make life as easy as possible for my pastor. It was maybe even just to make his day run more smoothly or efficiently. I wasn't bothered about seeing my own vision fulfilled because my vision was to see him succeed in his. An example of this was one night during a prayer meeting when someone shot one of our windows out with a pellet gun. Whilst 'the boss' carried on leading the prayer meeting, a friend and I released him from that burden by making sure everything was safe and screwing a piece of wood over the window. If we weren't there, he may have had to bring the prayer meeting to a close in order to deal with it himself.

KNOWLEDGE

Every now and again, you will find that God gives you a word of knowledge. This is a supernatural utterance from heaven into your inner being that highlights some information about a person or situation. This gift of knowledge can be a great faith builder and can be used to extend the kingdom of God in a special way.

I once heard of a man who would get invited into big businesses and corporations to prophesy over them. These corporations had heard of how God was using the man and felt it right to put a certain amount of trust in him to speak into their businesses.

The people of God are called to be a blessing to the nations. So if you have this gift, maybe you should try using it in a business or corporate setting.

MIRACLES

We might wonder why the gift of miracles is different from the gifts of healing. R. T. Kendall, in his new book, claims that they are different and that miracles are more akin to deliverance.[60] However, I'm not entirely sure that we can narrow it down to this alone. Instead I would want to look at the miracles that Jesus did.

When Jesus fed the five thousand, I'm sure it was considered a miracle. When he raised himself and others from the dead, I'm sure the people didn't say they were healed. They would have claimed a miracle had taken place. When Jesus walked on water, I bet his disciples thought they had just seen a miracle, and when he walked up to heaven, I'm sure they were wowed!

Maybe to work in the miraculous, then, is to perform signs and wonders that cause the heart and soul to release a "Wow!" Maybe you will be transported in the Spirit like Phillip, or you will raise someone from the dead like Heidi Baker. Maybe you will walk out of a high security prison with two broken legs like Brother Yun.

---

[60] R. T. Kendall, *Holy Fire*, 149-150.

TONGUES AND INTERPRETATION OF TONGUES

Some friends tell me that when people speak in tongues it scares them. It may be the case that you've sat in a church meeting and heard people speaking in what sounds like gobbledygook, and you may have felt a little uncomfortable. To be honest, I don't always trust people's motives when it comes to tongues; it seems to be the only gift of the Spirit that you can conjure up without his help. However, it is still a gift that is named in the Bible.

So what is it?

Tongues has three aspects to it. The first is said to be like a groaning from within, like your body has a deep need for the Spirit of God, and it begins to groan like your belly when it's empty. My experience of this is that I feel something like a chesty groan or an elongated grunt from within. Sometimes is sounds like a creaky door. My wife tells me that I do it my sleep, but it's different from snoring – which I do on a more regular basis too. In fact, she tells me off sometimes because I'll be doing it whilst we're watching TV together.

The second aspect of tongues is the vocal one. Some say that this is the language of the angels; almost like it's the heavenly language. It could be that this is the language that was spoken before the Tower of Babel. I often wonder if that's why they called it Babble! However, I've also heard stories in which people claim to have heard someone speak fluently in a foreign language, when that person believed they were speaking in tongues. This affirms what scripture says when tongues were heard for the first time. People from different nations asked how the uneducated disciples could speak in foreign languages as though they were natives.

A friend of mine used to speak in tongues all the time, and he used to say the same thing over and over again. Sometimes he even said it mockingly during games and stuff. I became quite annoyed because I thought it was fake, so when I got home one night I typed his exact phrase into Google's translation tool, and I was astonished to find that the words he was speaking were Persian and they meant, "Disturb the Baarth party," which at the time was Saddam Hussein's political party. Maybe next time I'll be less judgemental!

Finally, there is the interpretation of tongues. Sometimes when people speak in tongues they are actually prophesying into the room.

Rather than it being a heavenly sentence proceeding from the Spirit in you up to heaven, it is actually from heaven through the Spirit in you to the people in the room around you. Often these tongues can be interpreted by another Spirit-filled person in the room, and sometimes the person speaking in tongues has their own interpretation.

I've only ever interpreted tongues once or twice, but at the time, everyone else was speaking in tongues and I just felt like God started to say the same thing over and over again. In the same way as when I prophesy, I felt an overwhelming urge to speak out what I felt was God's voice inside. On one occasion it was actually a song, which isn't like me at all.

If you're worried about tongues, or if you have never spoken in tongues before, it could be quite hard for you to start. You might feel that people are going to laugh at you or that you'll sound stupid. This is all part of the Christian journey. You need to die to yourself and your pride and just speak out what God is putting in your head.

At first you may feel a bit shy and vulnerable, but once you've done it a few times you will start to feel an unusual emotion fill your stomach and work its way up to your throat. You may even get caught up in the euphoric feeling of joy as your whole body is overwhelmed by what feels like heaven touching earth.

I might never fully understand tongues, but I'm not sure that I have to. It's in the Bible so I think I'll just try to enjoy the mystery.

WISDOM

It's important that we understand the link between wisdom and knowledge, but that we also separate them in our minds. Whereas knowledge is the information that we know, wisdom is the gift that helps us to use that knowledge.

For example, just because you know that a member of your church is living in sin, it doesn't mean that you have to tackle it. Wisdom is using that knowledge well. Maybe that person is already having counselling with your pastor, and they need encouragement in the things that they are doing well this particular week. Tackling their sin just then would be a disaster and may bring to a halt the reconciliation process.

I always tell my guys that if they can follow instruction on the small things, I will give them bigger things to do with more responsibility. I believe it's the same with the Holy Spirit's wisdom.

1 Corinthians 7

CELIBACY

I don't believe that there are many people with this gift. I think that I may only know a few people with it and, if I'm honest, I'm not sure that they particularly want it or feel like they have it.

The Apostle Paul said that he chose to remain single so that family would not get in his way during his mission to reach the ends of the earth with the gospel. He even went as far as to say that he wishes that everyone would stay single, but I guess that might be a little bit of gift projection taking hold there (feeling that everyone should do what God has convicted us about). In another part of the Bible, however, Paul tells couples not to withhold themselves from each other, meaning that he wants couples to have sex. So maybe we can call celibacy 'singleness' too.

If you have the gift of singleness, you may still feel a deep need for companionship, but it is important that you recognise the difference between brotherly or sisterly affirmation and that of a sexual or lustful nature.

Often people with this gift might wonder if it is a lifelong gift, or if it is just for a season. They might also wonder why they feel a desire to be married even though they have this gift.[61] I would draw our attention to the fact that in society we have certain expectations over our lives and conduct. How we behave in society is called Social Psychology. If you were raised with the worldview that to be successful you need a wife, nice car, posh house and two children, then you may feel a desire to be affirmed in that way. My best advice is to seek God first for his affirmation, and all of your truest desires will be added to you.

---

[61] Barry Danylak, *On The Gift Of Singleness*, Boundaries, http://www.boundless.org/adulthood/2014/on-the-gift-of-singleness, accessed 27th February 2015.

From what I understand about this gift, people with it tend to feel the peace of God over their lives more intensely when they are single, and tend to feel uncomfortable spiritually when they are in a relationship. To some people it just comes naturally.

1 Peter 4

HOSPITALITY

If you're quite evangelistic in nature, you'll probably find that you are gifted with hospitality from the outset. This gift has a supernatural edge to it that a lot of people don't realise. Simply being nice to people and making cups of tea isn't the gift of hospitality.

When people spend time with me they tend to say that I make them feel comfortable, like they are a piece of the furniture. This is even the case when I enter someone else's home. I could come to your home for coffee and make you feel at peace and at home in your own home.

Recognising that I have this gift made me a lot bolder when visiting people at home as a pastor. I'm quite happy to ask people for a cup of tea, which gives me time to witness to family members and friends that might be round. In our Life Group sessions, the lads tend to feel a lot freer if I stretch out on the recliner sofa and put my feet up. It can often make the host of the meeting feel a little more comfortable too.

Making tea or coffee is nice, but the gift of hospitality is a supernatural Holy Spirit gift. If you have it, you must flaunt it. You will win more for Christ if you push the boat out a little. For example, with the recent issues facing Syria and other war-torn countries, you may find that the Spirit of hospitality will give you a heart to welcome in refugees. A friend of mine bought a house with three floors so that he could turn his bottom floor into a self-contained flat for a refugee family. You may also find that this gift is highlighted in your local church. Maybe you see many ways that your church community could better welcome people from outside. I am quick to notice new faces, and I always try to include people.

Some churches have a bad reputation for being cliquey. Such congregations would benefit from someone with the gift of hospitality to welcome new faces into their community, maybe even by inviting people round for dinner or including them in their group discussion.

1 Corinthians 13

MARTYRDOM

There's a saying, "The blood of the martyrs is the seed of the church!" What people mean by this is that the general history of persecution throughout the Jewish and Christian faith has proved to be one of its biggest building blocks of growth. Take for example the Hebrews in Egypt. They were taken as slaves and persecuted because they were blessed by God, and yet they carried on growing as a nation to the point that the ruler of Egypt felt his only option to stop his nation from being overrun by the Hebrews was to kill all of their baby boys.

Martyrs are those with the spiritual gift of being able to submit themselves to suffering for their faith – to the point of death. Their very outlook on death and suffering is different to that of the norm. Those who have this gift will be joyful in their persecution for the glory of God, and will often remain in persecution even if they have the means to escape.[62]

One great example of this is Brother Yun, who endured so much persecution it's almost unbelievable. In his book he states that whilst in prison he was made to clean out cesspits, but as that was the only place that the guards could not get to him, he used that time to worship God. This way he could worship his Saviour without being beaten by the prison guards.

Ephesians 3

MISSIONARY

Many people that go on mission these days tend to spend a few weeks or months in a foreign place doing good things. They often pay lots of money to go on missions trips, and will sometimes go once or twice a year. I'm not sure that this modern idea of missions is in line

---

[62] B. Embry, *Creative Suffering*, (USA; Xulon Press, 2005), 66.

with the biblical examples, or those shown by some of the world's most well known missionaries.

The Apostle Paul would spend anything from six months to a few years in a place, working as a tentmaker and serving the community, whilst living out the gospel in a way that people would see Jesus through his lifestyle. Of course he was an avid preacher and evangelist too, and many would come to faith through his ministry.

A modern example of this approach to mission is a lady called Jackie Pullinger, who spent the last of her money on a one-way ticket to China where she began to work among the locals. Her different lifestyle and her Holy Spirit gifting drew people to faith. Before long people would see the change in their friends' and family members' lives and many started to find faith in God.

The gift of the missionary, then, is the ability to cross cultural boundaries and give up your own life in order to be Christ in a culture that hasn't experienced him before. This gift is quite closely linked to the gift of voluntary poverty.

1 Corinthians 13

VOLUNTARY POVERTY

Paul said that he is content whether he is rolling in it or if he is poor. This is the heart of the man or woman with the gift of voluntary poverty. The only thing that I own is my car, and I'm happy with that. I wouldn't consider myself poor because I'm rich in spirit.

The core value of the person with this gift is that people (or the calling) matter more than money. Those gifted in this way will live a life of low dependency and be satisfied in whatever situation they find themselves financially.

To fan this gift into flame I would recommend decluttering your life. Find ways to lessen the faff in your routines. Shower in the evening so that you're ready to go if God calls you in the night. Get used to being organised and ready to do what God is calling you to do at the drop of a hat. You'll find it really rewarding if you remove all of the things in your life that could prevent you from following God into mission.

Ephesians 4

EVANGELISM

I once heard it said that there's a difference between being evangelistic and being an evangelist. I know many people who are evangelistic but whose ministry is not fruitful. It could be that their church leader is quite evangelistic and so they put a high value on this specific aspect of their Christian walk, or they might even have the gift of evangelism without receiving much training, which would then lead to them not showing fruit in their ministry.

It is, of course, vital to the church that people are encouraged to share their faith in ministry, but if you feel you have the gift of evangelism I would encourage you to find someone who actually bears the fruit of an evangelist to train you.

Very soon after committing to follow Christ, I felt that I was an evangelist. My friends and elders thought along the same lines, and my pastor would often bring in specialist teachers in evangelism to teach our church about the gift. When I went to Bible College I was mentored by an out-and-out evangelist who actually led people to Jesus on a regular basis. It wasn't until spending time with a fruitful evangelist that I began to lead people to Jesus.

Reading the Bible, I have seen the phenomenon of the 'laying on of hands' for a special spiritual anointing. For example, Elijah the prophet anointed his understudy, Elisha. Elisha went on to do the same signs and wonders as Elijah and pretty much carried on where he left off. With this in mind I have made it one of the core practices in my training to ask every fruit-bearing evangelist that I meet to lay their hands on me for their spiritual anointing. Whether you believe in this or not, I have found that since I started doing this I have literally led hundreds of people to Jesus. I have even had the honour of writing a Christmas article in The Sun newspaper. I preached the gospel to two and a half million readers.

Ephesians 4

PASTORAL CARE

In addition to the pastor, Christ's gift to the church, you do find in church life that there are pastoral types. Moreover, the theological interpretation of Ephesians 4 is that Christ gave the fivefold ministers to the church to train the church in their specific giftings. Logically this would imply that people who don't hold the office of Pastor could also be gifted with the supernatural gift to care for people pastorally.

So what does this gift look like? People who hold the office of Pastor have a specific fruit. Like the evangelist, whose fruit is seeing people receive salvation to follow Christ, the pastor's fruit in the church context is unity. People who are pastoral, however, have an innate longing to love people. They are loyal and form strong relationships. Sometimes they can accidentally form cliques, but their deepest desire is to please those around them. Sometimes these guys can be so people-centred that they don't get the task at hand done – but that's why we love them.

If you have this gifting, or any other gifting that is mentioned in this chapter, it would be a really good thing to find someone that knows about your gift, or has experience with it, to help you train. The church needs all of these gifts in operation, and the body of Christ wouldn't be the same if anyone was missing. However, as mentioned previously, Paul does instruct us to pray for the better gifts. For him, prophecy was quite high on his list, maybe because he was evangelistic. If you're pastoral, then maybe grace would be quite high on your list. Whatever the case, just remember that praying is never a bad thing, and all gifts from God are good.

7

Going Deeper

Spiritual maturity and the depth of your relationship with the Holy Spirit are not measured by what spiritual gifts you show but by the way you behave. We can see how close someone is to Father God when we see them acting like him. It's like when we spend a lot of time with someone and we begin to rub off on them, or they rub off on us. Sometimes we pick up their speech patterns and even their facial expressions. We begin to behave like them. In the Bible this is called the fruit of the Spirit.

If we born of God and have his 'DNA', we will begin to look like him and show the same supernatural power as him – but proof of our love for him will be the amount of time that we spend with him. Before long we will begin to pick up some of his characteristics.

To show more of God's characteristics in our lives we need to be even more consumed by his Spirit and his lifestyle. We need to make him the number one priority in our lives, and seek to be more like him. This is the essence of love! The more time we spend with him, the more his fruit will rub off on us.

In this chapter we will explore God's character – his core values or his fruit – and what it looks like in our everyday lives.

Love

In 1 Corinthians 13 the Apostle Paul tells his readers that if they show all of the gifts of the Spirit but don't show love then the miraculous is like a clanging cymbal – it's worthless! It's just noise and hype! Love is the characteristic of Christ that is the driving force behind everything that he has done since the beginning of time, when he created the world. Love should be the driving force behind everything that we do too. If the Spirit of God is our fuel, then love is the engine. Every other action or miraculous sign is merely the driveshaft that helps us to put the power to the wheels of journey with Christ.

If we claim to be filled with the Spirit of God but fail to show love, then we lie and we show that we are not truly at one with Christ.[63]

Some people believe that love is a feeling, but the truth is that love is actually a choice that we make. If we constantly rely on the physical manifestation of feelings to show us which routes to take in life, we'll leave ourselves open to spiritual confusion as the enemy of our souls can also manifest feelings within us. Take for example lust. Lust is the enemy of love! Satan wants you to be confused by a physical manifestation of a feeling that feels a lot like love but is actually out to ruin you.

Love, then, is a choice to show the other characteristics of Christ to your fellow man or woman despite what your feelings say. You may notice that the enemy can often create the strongest manifestations of hatred and envy, and cause you to want to act unfavourably towards those whom you have chosen to love. I find that the best way to counteract the enemy is to bring a rebuttal to his lies by voicing some of the praises that we give to Jesus. The Bible says that "faith comes through hearing", so if we quote scriptural praises for Jesus, like the names of God – King of Kings and Prince of Peace – then our praise will cause the devil to flee just like when Jesus went out into the desert in Matthew 4.

---

[63] 1 John 2:3-6.

Joy

Rick Warren, a well known pastor from America, says:

Joy is the settled assurance that God is in control of all the details of my life, the quiet confidence that ultimately everything is going to be alright, and the determined choice to praise God in every situation.[64]

Put another way, joy is the absence of worry and anxiety, meaning that you may be less worried about what people think of you or what's happening at home or in your finances. This may leave you subject to expressions of happiness and exultation, leaving you rejoicing or showing an outward pleasure or delight.[65]

One such example of this recently was in our church's annual holiday conference. As our guest speaker began to get stuck into talking about being open to the Holy Spirit, a lady began to giggle. Her laughing was infectious as it became louder and freer, eventually getting to a place where she was snorting with laughter and delight – free from the pressures of the world and anxiety about what others thought of her.

I've seen other people singing and dancing with joy, allowing themselves to be more expressive than they might normally be.

The way to become freer in the joy of the Holy Spirit is to separate your time of worship of God from your worries and fears. Allow yourself to be overcome by joy and focus only on him. Take a moment to do those things that make you feel insecure in your most joyous moments. This will break down the barriers that you might regularly experience between you and the joy that God wants you to live in.

---

[64] Daily Hope With Rick Warren, *The Definition of Joy*, http://rickwarren.org/devotional/english/the-definition-of-joy, accessed 26th August 2015.

[65] Collins English Dictionary, *Joy*, http://www.collinsdictionary.com/dictionary/english/joy, accessed 26th August 2015.

Peace

A dictionary definition of peace is 'to be free from disturbance'. In a church context this could mean choosing to stop thinking about work or an argument that you might have had with the wife at home. During the week, it could be leaving work in the workplace, or choosing to trust God with regard to your finances, meaning that you are not disturbed by them from day to day.

I've found that living in the peace that God has intended for us is a matter of choice. Just as with any of the fruits of the Holy Spirit, we need to choose to walk in the light of God's goodness for us. If you're addicted to drama, maybe you should check out what Peter says in 1 Peter 4:15-16:

> If you suffer it should not be as a murderer or a thief or any other kind of criminal, or even as a meddler. However, if you suffer as a Christian, do not be ashamed, but praise God that you bear that name.

The Message Bible (MSG) says:

> If they're on you because you broke the law or disturbed the peace, that's a different matter.

Peter is telling us that drama will always follow those that meddle in other people's business. A key ingredient to having a peaceful life is to keep your nose out of others' business and keep your mouth closed. If you want a peaceful life, you'll need to choose between that and a life full of drama.

Patience

Some preachers joke that the worst prayer you could pray is for patience, but I guess everyone has to pray for it at some point. Grace and patience go hand in hand though. It's impossible to have patience without grace. If you don't take offence when someone is late, or when they are making you frustrated, you should be able to hold your patience for a good deal of time.

One example of this was when I had agreed to take a friend to the hairdressers to have a knot taken out of their hair. I thought it was only going to be about ten minutes, so I took my children with me in the car. We were waiting there for a few hours and within about ten minutes the children were fighting and bickering. It was easy to be gracious towards my friend who is very close to us, and it was reasonably easy to let the kids bicker on as I knew that my own decisions had put us in that position. For sure the experience tested my patience, but afterwards I realised that grace and patience were a lot easier than I had previously thought them to be.

Before laying down my life and time for Jesus I used to lose my patience quite easily. The truth is that I *wanted* to because I thought it was my right to be angry and that people shouldn't treat me a certain way. Now that I've given my life over to Christ, I have given up my rights and chosen to live a life of love and patience.

Kindness

Kindness is a trait that you would think is really common among Christians, but when you look at the dictionary definition of 'kindness', you might be surprised. It means to be 'friendly, generous and considerate', yet Christians can be quick to form cliques and be inconsiderate of others. Sometimes the things we do in order to look like we're 'being good' can misfire and upset others. For example, a small group having a prayer meeting before a church service might look 'holy', but others who weren't invited could feel that those praying have been inconsiderate or unkind.

Kindness is about thinking before you act. It's about inviting everyone in a group to dinner and not just the two people that you like to hang out with. Kindness is about considering how others might feel when you write a certain comment or status update on Facebook. It isn't really about what we do; it's more about how others perceive what we do and how we should think about those things before going about our daily chores and tasks.

The best way to become more kind is to be more generous. Invite more people to be part of your group. Think before acting! I've learnt that I don't have to answer every question straight away. I can wait and think about the situations that I find myself in. I would hope that people perceive me to be kind.

Goodness

The word 'goodness' in the New Testament is often translated as 'virtue' which, when we think of it with regards to a woman's chastity, helps us to get a good idea of what goodness means. A woman's virtue speaks of her continuing moral upstanding. It talks of her reputation in her community and her commitment to her future lover. It's the fruit of an ongoing commitment to spiritual growth and maturity. It's not something you gain in a blink of an eye. It's something you earn the right to be called: a man or woman of virtue. N. T. Wright, British author and theologian, says:

> You could call it the power of right habits. You might say it was the result of many of years of training and experience. You could call it 'character' ... Ancient writers had a word for it: virtue.[66]

Virtue speaks of an established and stable lifestyle of goodness and good reputation. A life of discipline!

In the same way, our goodness speaks of our faith and our commitment to giving glory to God with our lifestyle. It is the fruit of a whole life that has been given over to showing our faith with our incorruptible moral behaviour.

Like the other characteristics of God, goodness is a choice. You don't keep your virtue by accident.

Faithfulness

Faithfulness relates to our commitment to God or to other people. It could relate to our commitment to a ministry or a church. It could be your commitment to your job. If you're faithful, you will stick around during the tough times. You will never be found sneaking off for an interview with another company during your lunch break, and head-hunters will be dealt the roughest of rebukes from you.

As a church leader I personally put faithfulness above most of the other fruits of the Spirit. I need my team to turn up when they've committed to. I need them to set a good example of how we put Jesus

---

[66] N. T. Wright, *After You Believe: The forgotten role of virtue in the Christian life,* (New York: Harper Collins Publisher Inc., 2010), 20.

and his mission above our own. I am thankful for my wife's faithfulness.

There was once a time, before I became a Christian, when my wife was worried whenever I walked out of the door. She was never sure when I was going to come home, or whom I was with. Today she no longer worries. Soon after I became a Christian, one of her friends asked why she wasn't worried about where I was anymore. Her answer was that she knew I was telling someone about Jesus.

The Holy Spirit in my life has made me more committed – faithful – to God's vision and to my wife.

Gentleness

As someone who doesn't come across as being particularly meek, it would be easy for me to say something like, "Meekness doesn't mean weakness!" However, my aim is to learn as well as teach about the Spirit of Jesus.

I was once told by an elder in my home church that I should be like an iron fist in a velvet glove. I have often heard the modern day parable of the man who owned a Ferrari and took joy in letting it purr as he cruised down the street, rather than speeding like a madman, trying to prove something.

Both of these examples speak of a level of self-control and awareness of the power that we carry. The story of Elijah the prophet comes to mind. He experienced the full power and presence of God in a small whisper once the loud, mighty storm that was raging outside had calmed down.

Meekness, then, could be seen as a quiet and soft strength – an awareness of the power and presence that we carry. We don't always need fireworks and drums or to shout our mouths off in order to get our point across. It's OK to think quietly in a world where you're expected to speak and act loudly.

Self-control

In a number of translations 'self-control' is called 'temperance'. It is certainly something that we all struggle with. Some people lose control loudly, and others do it quietly. Being so angry or frustrated that you cannot help but do something is not the way of the Spirit.

There are several things that you can do in order to become more self-controlled. Two of my own most effective ways of being more like Jesus are:

- *To not react with my mouth.*
  Choose not to say something when you feel angry or frustrated. Sometimes by waiting until you feel less emotional you can respond to the people around you in a better way. Certainly as a pastor I have to think before speaking on far more occasions. In times past I have been interviewed for TV and radio, and in that moment when you feel anxious and in the spotlight, it's very important to take a couple of breaths before answering each question.

- *To not act until the situation has passed.*
  There are times in life when we can react based on what someone else has said when they have lost control of their emotions. Sometimes it's good to allow them a chance to recant what they've said or done as this will reduce the risk of burning bridges with friends and colleagues.

  For example, someone might get angry at work and then react to their emotions by saying something insulting, or claim that they are leaving the company. This clearly isn't a good option for that person, their family or even for the company. We should save our reaction for a time when our emotions are under control. We shouldn't clear their desk and tell everyone on Facebook about how they've been rude to us. If you just wait and allow time for reconciliation, there's a good chance that your friend and colleague will still be around for years to come. It's easier to prevent a bridge from burning down than it is to rebuild one from scratch. Look after your relationships by praying for this spiritual fruit.

Humility

Philippians 2:4-11 tells us what biblical humility is, as shown through Jesus. Jesus didn't consider equality with God – or greatness

– something to be grasped at, or even aimed for. Jesus never lorded his awesomeness over people, but he stooped low and came under people to lift them up. His mission wasn't to conquer mankind, but to free mankind.

Humility is the exact opposite to conceitedness, in that if we are conceited we tend to feel that someone else shouldn't be lifted up and glorified. Christians in general are really bad at humility, and often come across as being conceited. So often I've heard people slagging off someone who sits on the front row with the pastor, or the new girl who gets to sing as part of the worship band. One person referred to me as the "blue-eyed boy" after my pastor asked me to sit with him once.

The best way to cultivate your humility is to first understand that you are a member of the royal family in heaven, and then to try to lift up those around you. Why not push someone else's agenda for once, get behind someone else's vision, serve them like Jesus would? When you see the results of it, you'll fall in love with the fruit of humility.

Finally, humility is being able to be humiliated. By this I mean that it's about not holding your own honour in high regard or making it a priority. Often we're most angered by people that dishonour us, but humility is being able to hang on a cross with no honour, stripped naked and having insults hurled at us, whilst breathing out the words, "Father, forgive them!" In my life this means that I can play the kids' games on the stage or sing karaoke at the church barbecue. If I'm totally honest, I have to die to my honour every time I get in the pulpit because I know there's always going to be someone that I offend.

Forgiveness

As a Christian you will hopefully have understood that one of God's most prevalent characteristics is that he is forgiving. Last week I did a school assembly on the subject of forgiveness and I described it as a burden that we carry around. As we trudge through the hills of life we might find that unforgiveness helps us during our downward spirals into depression and despair, and then it hinders us in our climb to our mountain top experiences.

Unforgiveness can have a massive impact on our lives, and yet it doesn't affect the person that we are being unforgiving towards. They don't feel the burden of your unforgiveness, and it certainly doesn't cause them sleepness nights or despair.

I'm often asked how we can learn to forgive those that have hurt us, and I believe you can do it in two ways. There is an emotional response to unforgiveness and a physical response too. The emotional response is to pray for those whom you have issues with. The Bible actually says that you will heap coals on their head as you pray blessings over them,[67] but this shouldn't be the reason for your prayers. As you pray, you will begin to love that person.

The physical response to bring about forgiveness is to make an effort to be a better friend. Try buying them a gift or blessing them in some other way. I told the children in our assembly to think about inviting those people to be part of their game or their group. This is a sure-fire way to find forgiveness for those who have hurt you.

Courage

As a Christian, in Western culture, we need to be courageous in ways that are different to Christians elsewhere in the world. For example, in places like the Middle and Far East you can be putting your life and physical wellbeing on the line for the sake of the gospel. For this reason, followers of Jesus need to be courageous and show strength in the face of fear. Here in the UK we don't risk our lives for our faith, but we risk social exclusion, a way of life, or a job for the sake of Jesus.

It's in the midst of this risk that we face a very real social fear. If you read my first book, Chav Christianity, you'll know that in a working class environment people are your greatest asset or possession. So the very notion of risking losing friends and family over choosing to follow Christ can fill a person with a lot of fear.

This is where we need courage. Courage isn't the absence of fear, it is the ability to face our fears and follow what's right even during adversity. Courage is saying no to peer pressure, or sharing your faith with your family. Courage is making a choice to pray for your family

---

[67] Romans 12:20.

or friends when they are hurting, or even when they're not, despite the fear of losing them. Courage in a hostile context is choosing to follow Christ, even though it could mean death, torture or imprisonment.

The beauty of courage is that, like most other fruits or gifts of the Spirit, you can grow it like a muscle. The more you use it, the stronger it becomes. The more you stand up to fear, the less it affects you. The Bible says, "Resist the devil and he will flee."[68] In the same way, if we resist fear it will eventually stop holding us captive!

Honesty

Honesty and accountability is an important part of a Christian's life, for the sake of their discipleship and for their relationship with God and other Christians. However, there is a fine line between being honest and over-sharing. It is socially normal to let someone know that you are having a bad day, but it is not very good social etiquette to tell people all of the ins and outs of your day.

Over-sharing can lead to relationships that peter out very quickly due to high intensity, but honesty can build depth into relationships like nothing else. Honesty is the moderate characteristic that sits between secretive and over-sharing.

Honesty is a particularly good characteristic to possess when it comes to building our relationship with God too, although there's no better place to over-share than at the mercy seat. Jesus is a friend that you can trust, and he encourages us to lay our burdens at his feet to be free from the worries of life.

Gratitude

Having a spirit of gratitude is a great asset for a fulfilled life. It breeds positivity and makes a person a joy to be around. 1 Thessalonians 5 says:

Rejoice always, pray continually, give thanks in all circumstances; for this is God's will for you in Christ Jesus.

---

[68] James 4:7.

Some people are naturally more optimistic and others more pessimistic. It is unlikely that you will be able to change your basic personality. However, it is possible to change your mind-set and train yourself to do almost anything, including having an attitude of gratitude.

As well as praying for this fruit of the Spirit, I would recommend that you read some books on positive psychology. There is a great book by Albert Ellis called 'How to Stubbornly Refuse to Make Yourself Miserable About Anything Ever'.[69] In the book he explains that we can all choose to change our attitude by giving up certain belief systems. For example, if there is an incident (I), for example someone taking our seat in church, and our reaction (R) to it is anger, then the link between the incident and our reaction is our belief (B) – in this case, that someone shouldn't sit in our 'normal seat' at church. He claims that in order to remove the negative reaction (R) we must first change our belief (B).

In short, we can train ourselves to be more positive and thankful by removing negative beliefs or characteristics, like arrogance or a sense of entitlement.

Responsibility

Jesus showed an intense awareness of his own responsibility in the Garden of Gethsemane when he prayed to Father God, "Not my will but yours…"[70] Unfortunately, we live in a blame culture where many do not take responsibility for their own lives. We blame other people for a lack of provision or opportunity, and I've even heard people blame God for putting temptation in their way. However, we have a responsibility for ourselves and our actions. In fact, the fruit of faithfulness is very much coupled with responsibility as we are told that "each of us will give an account of ourselves to God" in Romans 14. You choose when you quit or when you take offence. I believe that 'responsibility' is the missing characteristic from our postmodern culture. If we are to see a breakthrough in the Western church, we

---

[69] Citadel Press, 1988.
[70] Luke 22:42.

will need Christians to stand up and be counted for longer than a month at a time.

Contentment

One of my favourite Bible passages is Philippians 2. Humility and contentment go hand-in-hand in this chapter, as in most of life. Jesus is described as being content with his standing with God, in that he didn't consider equality with God something to be grasped. He was content being the face of love as he chose to be the sacrifice that the Jews so badly needed in order to feel pure and forgiven. The Bible says that he gave up heaven by choice in order to live and die for a race that, for the most part, would deny him.

Paul, filled with the Spirit, said that he was content in all situations.[71] Whether poor or rich we can find joy is just being at one with our creator – free to enter his presence at any time, or even to live in that presence.

Finding contentment in life means to be comfortable with who God has made us to be, and to find fulfilment in what God has called you to do.

Generosity

In Acts 2 we see the church – a group of disciples of Jesus – baptised in the Holy Spirit for the first time. After the writer chronicles the Apostle Peter's preach to the masses, he explains the first thing that happens among believers when they received the Spirit:

> *All believers were together and had everything in common. Selling their possessions and goods, they gave to anyone as he had need.*[72]

Living a generous life is the Christian way. Jesus literally gave everything up so that he could meet with us. He was more bothered about our eternity than his wealth or power. To cultivate this fruit of the Spirit I tend to be willing to give stuff away no matter what.

---

[71] Philippians 4:11.
[72] Acts 2:44-45.

One day recently I was feeling really hungry. I hadn't had a chance to eat during the day because I was running around doing pastoral work. I finally managed to get a few minutes to eat when someone else turned up at my door in the early afternoon. I took the person for a road trip to collect some furniture, but by the time we collected it I was feeling a little worse for wear. In my hunger I was starting to dislike this person, but the Holy Spirit in me gave me the ability to be like Christ. Buying myself a sandwich at the local shop, I was urged to share it with the person that had kept me from my late lunch. That day I felt a supernatural sort of love as I gave out of my 'poverty'.

The best way to cultivate this fruit, then, is to keep giving no matter who the person is that you are giving to, or no matter how poor you are.

Compassion

Six times the Gospels record that Jesus showed "compassion". In most instances it was towards a large crowd of people. And it was Jesus' compassion that led him to the cross.

The word 'compassion', when used in Matthew 9:36, means 'to be moved in one's bowels'. You may be able to remember a time when you felt a deep sense of pity and love for someone, in such a way that your stomach felt like it had been turned inside out. It is this gut-wrenching love and pity that Jesus is feeling when he feels compassion towards you. The people of New Testament times believed that the bowels were the seat of love and pity.[73]

The way that you cultivate this fruit of Jesus' character is to succumb to it. Let yourself be bound by this burden, even though at times it may hurt. I sometimes get a prophetic pain for people that I pray for.

Once I saw a young man in our church. I felt an awful pain in my stomach, and felt like rather than this being a pain that he felt, it was actually a pain that God felt for the young man. I approached him and explained how God felt about him. It's only now that I can put a name to that pain: *compassion!*

---

[73] Strong's Greek, *4697. splagchnizomai*,
    http://biblehub.com/greek/4697.htm, accessed 30th November 2015.

Obedience

I have personally been working on obedience since very soon after becoming a Christian. Over seven years of just saying yes, it has become easier and easier. In fact, I can probably count the times that I've said no to God – and felt like rubbish for a number of days afterwards! I often tell our church that the easiest way to be obedient to God, and see the miraculous in our life, is to get into the habit of saying yes to him. It's that simple. Even if you feel embarrassed, just remain obedient. Obviously, you may need to choose your words carefully if you're in certain places or situations though.

Grace

You may recall that we mentioned grace as a gift of the Spirit – one of the elements of God's power in us – but it's also a characteristic of Jesus, and can be part of your character too. In John 1:14 the Bible tells us that Jesus is full of grace. Here we can see that Jesus has a natural inclination to show favour and positivity towards the people around him. You might say that he always thinks the best of believers, or that his natural instinct is to look at the good in people.

The Bible says the same about Father God. On the day of judgement, he won't even notice our wrongs because they have been totally washed away by the blood of Jesus. When weighing our good against our bad, he will only count our good. Jesus spoke of a refiner's fire that removes all of our wrongs, as far as the east is from the west. When God looks at you right now, he only sees the positive.

You too can have a default position of positivity towards your friends and family. Jesus gives to us whether we are going to waste his gift or not. Maybe next time you see a homeless man in the street you will just give out of grace, rather than letting the enemy put doubts of worthiness and waste in your mind.

Being Childlike

Being childlike does not mean being childish; rather it means having faith like a child; being open to the spiritual and quick to believe, almost a little naïve when it comes to what God is telling us to do. If knowledge puffs up, then childlike faith is a key to humility.

This characteristic is the beautiful ability to be able to put your brain to one side and follow God; after all, the Bible says that God uses the foolish things of this world to confound the wise.

One of my favourite examples of this characteristic of Christ is Heidi Baker. I love the way that she explains her faith in a way that a Sunday school pupil can comprehend. She finds such joy in just showing love to people, whether they follow Christ or not. I love her tears as she extends the hand of God to those in need. For Heidi Baker, ministry is less about theory and more about just following the Holy Spirit's lead into whatever situation he desires.

Creative

God has a creative personality. He loves it! He loves to be praised for his creative prowess. Many worship leaders, artists, and creative types might be gobsmacked that it has taken this book so long to get to their favourite and most exciting characteristic of God! For people that pray for healing – asking for God to re-create lungs or ligaments – this is the most powerful attribute of Father God. For contemplatives, who love to encounter God in nature, this virtue is the most amazing.

I love to see people dance, paint or play instruments during worship, showing love to their creative God in their own individual way. Let me be the person to say, express yourself! God loves it! He thinks it's very good!

Being Disciplined

Living a disciplined life is the essence of discipleship. Some of us find discipline very comforting as we journey with Christ and others, whereas for many this isn't the case. Jesus had twelve close disciples and thousands of others, so he clearly considers this an important virtue to have.

They say that if you do something for forty days it will become a habit, and I have made it a priority in life to replace bad habits with good ones. Most recently I began making an effort to kneel and pray before I get into bed each night. At first I had to try hard to remember to do it each night, but a few months on it became natural. For others it might be praying every morning before starting your day. Still other people might aim to do a kind deed for another person each day, or to smile at a stranger.

Integrity

Integrity is a lot like honesty, but it revolves around your actions and lifestyle more than around what you say. For example, a preacher once gave a lecture at our Bible college, and he said that for him integrity is about dressing the same way on Sunday morning as he does at the family barbecue on a Saturday afternoon. By which he meant that to have integrity is to be the same person all of the time; not wearing a mask. It is the opposite of hypocrisy.

Unfortunately, some people portray a different person at the office or at home than the one they show off at church or in front of their Christian friends. It is important to be the same person in your internet history as the one you are in church.

My prayer is that the church would put a higher value on integrity as a fruit of the Spirit. Jesus never stopped being God when he became part of his creation. He remained Love and Grace. Even when confronted with death, he answered, "I AM," and he is the same yesterday, today and forever.[74]

Zealous

Finally, Jesus is so passionate about you that his passionate love can be described as zealous. 'Zealous' can also be translated 'jealous'.

Let me paint you a picture of God's love for you. Have you ever been in love with a member of the opposite sex? Let's say you are married and you notice that another man looks at your other half with the sort of eyes that you might consider doting. You may feel an intense feeling of jealousy for your wife. Imagine if that man then approaches your wife to say hello. Let me tell you, at that point my intense jealousy might begin to turn into an angry rage.

Jesus saw the enemy looking at us with lustful, hateful eyes from the beginning of time, but instead of getting angry he decided on a

[74] Mark 14:62. See also the seven 'I AM' sayings of Jesus: John 6:35, 8:12, 10:9, 10:11, 11:25, 14:6, 15:1.

way to show his perfect love and devotion to us. Every time we begin to look back to sin, Jesus' heart starts to beat faster, he feels jealous and pained by our interaction with it. He is passionate about us and our wellbeing. Maybe if we let this notion of zealous love that Christ has for us sink in, we will begin to feel the same way in return.

It's a zealous love for Christ that drives us to work on all of these characteristics of his personality. This zealous love drives us to want him more, to want to wait in his presence for hours, days, months on end. In chapter 9 we will look at ways in which we can learn to walk in his presence.

8

Upsetting Him

Ephesians 4:30 says:

> *Do not grieve the Holy Spirit of God, with whom you were sealed for the day of redemption.*

There is no single consensus amongst Christian regarding what this means, and there has been much debate. With that in mind my aim here is to give you hope if you have lost it, and maybe to clarify a few points, although I don't claim to know everything about this subject.

Like a Dove

The Bible paints a picture of the Holy Spirit as being like a dove. In the account of Jesus' baptism in water, it says that the Holy Spirit came to rest on him. I have heard it said that the Holy Spirit comes and goes like a bird, but for the most part I think this isn't true. The Bible says that we are *sealed* with the Holy Spirit, like an engagement ring that shows all who see us that we belong to God. The image of the dove, then, is to show the *gentleness* of the Holy Spirit.

One snowy afternoon, I visited a man who delivered bibles for the Gideons I was picking up some furniture from his home to give to the poor. Whilst we were there, my team and I were offered a hot drink and a chance to meet his doves. They were kept in his garage whilst it was snowing to keep them warm. As he opened his garage these shy and gentle birds walked and hopped out into the snow. Doves are very shy at first, and take very tentative steps towards you, but if you are gentle too, they are happy to come and eat from your hand or even sit on you. Sudden jerks can frighten them, but for the most part they are very sociable birds and they like to settle down. Once you have homed a bird in your dovecote for a few weeks, they will not fly away. That will be their home for years to come.

So, once the Holy Spirit comes he is very reluctant to leave. Actually, he's so reluctant to leave that not even your sin will make him leave. If you're open to him teaching you and guiding you, he will keep on nudging you towards Jesus until judgement day when all sin and unrighteousness will be washed away anyhow.

The Holy Spirit is your closest friend and companion. He is on your side and he wants the best for you. If we see him as a dove, then we must learn from this that once he finds his home in you, he is very unlikely to move on or be scared away for any reason.

Ignoring Him

Ignoring the Holy Spirit can have dire consequences. From time to time you will be tempted by the enemy, or even by your own ambition and desires. But the Holy Spirit will guide you, using your emotions, people around you or the Bible, into a righteous lifestyle. It is possible to ignore him though, and you are even able to drown out his voice. Doing this to someone would clearly upset them, but the good news is that God is bigger than us. He's more mature than us, and he's more committed than us. Just think, if God was willing to literally die for you in a torrent of abuse and torture, then there's a really good chance that he can cope with you ignoring him. Unfortunately for you, though, this could lead to a rubbish life, and could even bring you a place where you think that God is not at work in your life.

If you've ever thought, "Why is my life a mess? Where are you, God?" it could be that you have drowned out the voice of the Holy Spirit in order to seek worldly pleasure or acceptance. However, you can always go back to the beginning. Remember, Jesus asked the church in Revelation to remember their first love. You just need to get back to him.

Lying to Him

There is this a story in the New Testament of two of the followers of The Way – the Christian faith – called Ananias and Sapphira. They gave an offering to the church in order to see that the poor were fed. According to scripture they claimed that they had given more than they actually had done. The Bible says that they literally keeled over and died; that God killed them for lying to his Holy Spirit. Now that sounds scary! Having said that, this seems to be the only time that such an event happened in scripture, and I don't believe it has happened since.

It's a bit like Peter walking on water. It happened that one time, and everyone has tried to walk on water since – especially if you're a bit flamboyant like me. However, I have not heard of any another instance of this miracle.

Lying to the Holy Spirit is clearly a bad thing to do, but then so is spitting in the face of the Saviour for most of your life. If God can forgive you for a lifetime of sin that has been recorded against him and everyone else, then I'm sure God can forgive you for lying to him. Be warned, though; you could be the next person to keel over!

Disowning Him

The Bible says that if we disown Jesus in front of men, then he will disown us in front of the Father. I often have conversations about whether you can lose your salvation or not and, if I'm totally honest, I'm not really sure. I think that people can be really judgemental, and that sometimes when we see that a friend or colleague has stopped attending church – sometimes because they feel that they connect better with God in other ways, or they feel that there isn't a church that fits their need – we can jump to the conclusion that they have disowned God or that they are no longer Christians. As a result, we may say that they have lost the Holy Spirit's presence in their life, but I think that this is going a bit far.

The only real consequence of missing out on church life would be that you lose a large part of the discipleship process, by not being part of the community. Psychologists say that most people are conformed to the dominant culture that they surround themselves with, so if you choose to leave church and surround yourself with godless people, you may begin to behave in a godless way. You won't reap the benefits of being part of God's family. You may make more silly mistakes, such as having affairs or becoming addicted to something. However, you won't lose the Holy Spirit.

The scriptures that talk about disowning Jesus are meant to encourage people to stay strong during times of persecution. Look at Peter! He disowned Jesus three times, but in Luke 22 Jesus told Peter that even though this would happen, he would pray for Peter to be able to strengthen his brothers when he returns to Christ.

Hebrews 6: Nothing is Impossible with God

The book of Hebrews was written to a heavily persecuted church that were falling away left, right and centre. The Romans and Jews were so hard on them that they had to hide everything they did.

Hebrews 6 draws a picture of how a person can bring things into their life and renounce the Holy Spirit and ignore him, eventually leading to a separation from God even after being so close to him that they could almost taste of his goodness. If you can imagine that your sin is a wall between you and God, by confession and faith in Jesus you can knock that wall down before it becomes a blockage between you and the Father. You might imagine that by disowning Christ, lying to him and ignoring him, you would begin to stop confessing to have your slate wiped clean. You might even begin to start making excuses as to why you need your sin more than you need his forgiveness. This is a really dangerous thing to do because Hebrews 6 says that if you fall away, Christ will not go to the cross for you again. It will be to his shame if he has to bail you out again. If your bricks get so high that you choose to walk away for good, there's a really good chance that your pride in sin may stop you from ever coming back.

The good news, though, is this:

With man this is impossible, but with God all things are possible.[75]

Although, sometimes, getting back to God may seem impossible, he is sold out for you and always has been. He wants you to be part of his life and for him nothing is impossible.

---

[75] Matthew 19:26.

9

Staying Connected

We've talked about connecting with God's Spirit and we've looked at who he is and what he does, as well as how he interacts with us. In this chapter we'll discuss how we can *stay* connected with the Holy Spirit.

You'll be glad to know that you can experience the goodness of God's presence in many different places and ways. You don't need to fly halfway around the planet to find a revival meeting, or move into a monastery, although these are both options.

A book that I have found to be very helpful on this topic is Sacred Pathways[76] by Gary Thomas. I struggled to understand other Christians until I read this book, at which point I started to see faith through different eyes. I've also tried to become more rounded, seeking out different ways to connect with God. This is where the journey really begins.

Meditation Techniques

Many 'generals of the faith' who have lived in years past have shown us the importance and intimacy of meditation. I think of St Julian of Norwich who spent perhaps forty years of her life hidden away in a cell of solitude where her obsession was in meeting with

---

[76] Zondervan (2010)

the risen Christ.[77] Consider also St John of the Cross, who lived a life of poverty, penance and prayer to the point where he was so used to the Spirit's manifest – almost physical – presence that he made a name for the times when he wasn't walking in it: the dark night of the soul!

Then there was Francis of Assisi who amazingly tried to steal some cloth and a horse from his father's shop in order to sell them and raise money for the church. Upon hearing what his son had done, the father dragged Francis to the local bishop, who told the young man to return the money to his father. Francis gave his father all of the money, and then proceeded to strip naked and give his clothes to his father too, claiming that he would no longer recognise him as his father, but instead would only recognise God to be his father. Francis then gave his whole life over to living in poverty and preaching the gospel. Today, people who follow the order of St Francis tend to live in communities that share possessions, responsibility and resources. They are often known for their robes and lifestyle of poverty.[78]

Meditation means to dwell on something. The Ignatian practice of Lectio Divina in its most basic form is to dwell on a passage of scripture. The idea is that you read a portion of scripture several times, then pause, and maybe even have a short burst of sleep. You repeat the process, sometimes for hours, and listen to God's voice as he connects with you. Calvin Miller, writer of 'Loving God Up Close', writes:

> *When the brain speeds up to 9-14 cycles per second, the Alpha state, the person is enjoying some healthy sleep. When the brain speeds up to 15-40 cycles per second, the Beta state, the person has reached a state of creative rest. The Beta state is true Sabbath. We are in his presence and*

[77] L. H. McAvoy, *A Companion To Julian Of Norwich*, (Rochester: Boydell & Brewer Inc., 2008), 19.
[78] The Society of Saint Francis, *Life in Community*, http://www.franciscans.org.uk/living-as-franciscans/life-in-community, accessed 2nd December 2015.

*at peace. Here we are so "with God" that our conversation
with him is entire. We are rapt in oneness with God.*[79]

So when we spend time meditating, dwelling on and in God's presence, sometimes not even thinking about much at all, God is able to speak to us in a clearer and more intimate way. Meditation, then, is about dwelling in the rest of God, seeking his intimacy, not his power or knowledge.

Serving

One of my favourite ways to encounter God is when I'm serving him. Sometimes it could be when I'm doing a menial, boring task that's quite repetitive. This is a lot like meditating.

Once I was painting some racking in our charity warehouse in Northampton. I was almost in a trance-like state just painting this metal racking and thinking about the Bible. I thought, "What did Jesus mean when he said that he had come to fulfil the law?" I thought about this for what seemed like hours and felt that God spoke to me. As the day went on, I sensed I was standing in God's presence, interacting with him as I served him.

Some preachers might tell you of the exhilarating manifest presence of God as they go on a 'Holy Spirit rant' as they're preaching. This Sunday as I approached the pulpit to speak I noticed that it was a little cold. So I looked at one of heaters to see if it was switched on. The light was on but no heat was coming out because the heaters hadn't been turned up. I felt God's presence as we began to look at the Bible account of the withered fig tree.[80] God was certainly with us and was speaking to us through our heating not working. It was ace!

Gary Thomas calls us the activists. We encounter God through action. Unfortunately, sometimes we can feel as though people aren't 'real Christians' if they don't have our fervour to serve God. Be warned that this is an easy way to alienate people.

---

[79] C. Miller, *Loving God Up Close: Rekindling your relationship with the Holy Spirit,* (USA: Warner Books, 2004), 11.
[80] Matthew 21:19.

Worship

The Bible says that God inhabits the praises of his people. Some people would say that this is a promise of God as well as a reality of who God is and what he's all about. My personal experience is that this is totally true, even if there is only one of his people singing his praises. Some of my most intense times of meeting with God and feeling the power of his Spirit are during times of worship, whether that's whilst driving along listening to my favourite worship CD, or as part of what many call a 'glory tunnel'.

Let me explain what a glory tunnel is. I was once in a CFAN[81] meeting in Birmingham NEC, a huge venue used for music gigs and famous comedians. During one of the sessions of this conference, Reinhard Bonnke and his team asked all of the pastors in the room to come forward and stand in parallel lines, forming a tunnel – a glory tunnel. As over four thousand people walked through this 'tunnel', pastors were asked to pray for everyone to be filled with God's Spirit, and prophesy over them if they could. I saw one man having to be carried towards the end of the tunnel because the presence of God was so real and powerful.

Another time that I felt God's awesome presence like this was during a prayer meeting at a small church near to Tewkesbury. I used to drive about thirty to forty minutes every Tuesday evening to run a prayer meeting for the people there. On this one occasion I was the only person to turn up. I knelt at the front of church and just prayed for what seemed like an hour. I cried for the church and the neighbourhood that we were in. I prayed for the young people and the elderly. I prayed for the leadership there and for the finances. Finally, I heard a knock and looked up. It turned out that the whole time an elder had snuck in and was sitting next to me whilst I was blubbing. On the way home the presence of God was so tangible that I closed my eyes as I drove down the motorway. I had to open my eyes again because I felt sure there was someone in the car with me. I was as though I could hear the Spirit of Jesus breathing next to me.

---

[81] Christ For All Nations.

Learning

My wife is very intellectual. In fact, she's far cleverer than me. Sometimes when I talk about the way that God stirs my emotions, Laura can be a little indifferent. This is because God has made us all in different ways; she will find God moves her when she learns something really significant, like a link between something that King David said and the New Testament, such as Psalm 22. You may find yourself feeling like an outsider when people are connecting with God on an emotional level near you and you fail to feel him, but rest assured, you probably just connect with God in a different way.

The Bible says that we should be transformed by the renewing of our *minds,* so there's hope for those that struggle to feel but love to think. God created us with brains that can experience him in a great and unique way. There is so much goodness in the Bible from front to back that we can be blown away every day if we like to read. Take for example the moment that you're reading Genesis 28 and you see that Abraham claims that God will provide a lamb for the slaughter, yet when we read on we see that God provides a ram caught by its horns in a thicket. When you then learn that some theologians believe that mountain to be the one that Jesus, the Lamb of God, was sacrificed on... your mind is blown![82] Amazing.

As we walk closer to the Holy Spirit through everyday life, he begins to teach you in all kinds of ways. You begin to think like him and think with him. Let him teach you. The more you allow him to mould you, the more he'll get involved. In church, if you ask an actively involved person to do a job, you know they'll do it. Maybe it's the same in heaven! God uses those who are open to being used. God teaches those that are open to being taught.

Community

Community is an interesting concept, and I've found that in intense times of community God does big things quickly. I've found that God loves community.

---

[82] See, for example, Anthony Charles Garland, *A Testimony of Jesus Christ*, page 362, ISBN: 0978886429.

Psalm 133 says:

How good and pleasant it is when God's people live together in unity!

I have also found, in church leadership, that after times of living together people always come away saying that they met with God in a much more real way. Recently I had two people approach me to ask if they could become members of the church and start tithing, just after a week-long conference where they lived in the same house as the rest of the church family. The best thing was that we had not addressed either subject during the week.

Dietrich Bonhoeffer is one of the champions of Christians living in community together. Where some may find that they are able to connect with God easier during times of solitude, Bonhoeffer and people like him would argue that they find the warm embrace of a brother in Christ can break the deadlock of presence that they so eagerly long for. Without interaction with the body of Christ we will never know the truth of love, of grace or of intimacy.

Bonhoeffer once wrote:

Nothing can be more cruel than the leniency which abandons others to their sin. Nothing can be more compassionate than the severe reprimand which calls another Christian in one's community back from the path of sin.[83]

Even more powerful was Bonhoeffer's understanding of forgiveness. He said:

I can no longer condemn or hate a brother for whom I pray, no matter how much trouble he causes me.[84]

Praying for enemies so that God will heap coals on their head[85] is very different to praying for someone in your community that you struggle to get along with for the sake of love and community. Unfortunately, we will never know this love and unity unless we make

---

[83] D. Bonhoeffer, *Life Together*, (Norwich: SCM Press, 1988), 83.
[84] Bonhoeffer, *Life Together*, 65.
[85] See page 90.

a point of *living in community* for the sake of Jesus. It is in these times that God squeezes you like a sponge that is being dipped in the water, which represents the Holy Spirit's presence. Unless you are squeezed you won't be saturated. How squeezable are you?

Creation

I had a friend at Bible College who used to walk through the beautiful grounds of our head office chatting to God. I always thought it was a bit weird because he would walk along talking out loud, having a conversation with the Holy Spirit as though he was walking beside him.

Recently I found a new friend who loves to ride her bike out to a certain field with a tree it. There she feels God's presence more than she ever does in a loud worship service. In fact, it's as if she's seen a revival breakthrough in her spiritual life recently. It's quite an amazing story from someone who has been around church for many years and yet has never experienced the fullness of God in the way that she does in the middle of this field.

God is clearly creative and enjoys creation. Genesis tells us that God likes to walk among his creation,[86] so what better place to accidentally bump into him? The fact that he goes to the lengths of creating such intricate and delicate flowers or birds says that he is clearly interested. As we're made in the image of God, it makes sense for us to find excitement, passion and glory in both being creative and spending time amongst his creation.

What's more, you may also find historic buildings a good place to find God. Living in Lincoln, we are lucky to have one of the UK's largest and most beautiful cathedrals on our doorstep. Actually, it's on top of the only hill for miles around. You can practically see the cathedral from anywhere in our city, and at night it is lit up so you can see it from far outside of the city. I sometimes like to imagine what Solomon's Temple would have looked like with the intricate flowers and strong pillars, often becoming lost in the wonder and mystery of God.

---

[86] Genesis 3:8.

Prayer

After becoming a Christian, I joined three prayer meetings that took place every week. One was a men's prayer meeting on Friday nights, and I heard God's audible voice there on one occasion. I had my first visions, my first theological debates, and my first upset in the church community during those prayer meetings. I also saw some of my first miracles and answered prayers. I still find that one of my favourite ways to experience the Holy Spirit and grow in intimacy with him is to get into a decent prayer meeting.

My advice would be push yourself to stay longer. Nowadays I don't really feel like I'm getting started in a prayer meeting until I've been there for two or three hours. I would also recommend finding a comfortable place to fall asleep. I thought to myself that I should at least stay awake for an hour, mainly because I felt guilty after what Jesus said to his disciples in the Garden of Gethsemane. One day I felt like I was nodding off and I was fighting it, telling God that I wouldn't let him down during the prayer meeting; but then I felt I heard him say that it was OK to fall asleep on this occasion. I had the most amazing vision of God in heaven, and since then I am less concerned about falling asleep in God's presence, and I sometimes even welcome the restorative peace that God brings.

There's no better place to fall asleep and rest than in the glorious power and presence of God.

Walking in His Presence

I have found, in my time as a Christian, that it is possible to walk in the presence of God at all times. Many Christians look for a special service or a famous preacher to 'stir up the atmosphere' in a way that opens them to God's presence, but in fact it is possible to know his presence as you pop round a friend's house for a cup of coffee, or even whilst you're waiting in the garage for your car to be fixed.

One day a young man from church rang me up to ask if I could help him move a sofa. When I got to his house, the lad's neighbour came over to say hi. I noticed that she had a tracheotomy in her throat, and asked if it was uncomfortable. She replied by saying that it *was* uncomfortable, but that it wasn't *meant* to be. Sensing that God was near and going to do something, I asked her if it was bleeding, to which she again replied with a yes. It was actually infected. She had been suffering with throat cancer and had stopped drinking alcohol and was trying to quit smoking. I asked her if I could pray for her at my mate's house. It was lunchtime on a normal Tuesday afternoon, and as we prayed, I didn't feel particularly overwhelmed by the Spirit's presence. A couple of weeks later the lady rang our church asking for a food parcel. When I went to her house with a Foodbank voucher I asked her how her throat was. Apparently she had gone to the doctor who, after examining her throat, had told her that she had been healed and that she should be able to have her tracheotomy removed.

Sometime later, I met up with her cousin who lives in our neighbourhood. He asked me if I was the pastor that had prayed for his cousin, and confirmed that she had been healed. Moments like this are great and really get your faith fired up.

Dark Night of the Soul

We become so used to walking in God's presence that when, like a dad, he takes his hands away to let us walk on our own feet, we can feel almost like part of us has died. My experience of this 'dark night of the soul' is that at times it has felt as though God has removed his awesome power and presence from me. These have been some of the most depressing, scary and dark times in my journey with Christ. I began to wonder what I had done to scare God away or to upset him. I doubted myself and my salvation. However, I dug in! I looked for more ways to encounter God. I searched for him more. I cried!

I once heard Bill Johnson, a famous American preacher and church leader, say that the difference between religion and relationship is that religion always tries to find God the way that it did before, whereas relationship seeks to experience the love of God in new ways every day.

The good news for me, and maybe for you right now if you're going through this dark night of the soul, is that his presence is renewed.